JAPAN AND EDUCATION

Japan and Education

Michael D. Stephens

Robert Peers Professor of Adult Education
University of Nottingham

St Martin's Press New York

All rights reserved. For information write:
Scholarly and Reference Division
St. Martin's Press, Inc., 175 Fifth Avenue,
New York, N.Y. 10010

First published in the United States of America in 1991

Printed in Hong Kong

ISBN 0-312-05221-9

Library of Congress Cataloguing-in-Publication Data
Stephens, Michael Dawson
Japan and education / Michael D. Stephens.
    p. cm.
Includes index.
ISBN 0-312-05521-9
1. Education—Economic aspects—Japan.   2. Education and state–
–Japan—History.   3. Economic development—effect of education on.
I. Title.
LC67.J3S74   1991
370'.952—dc20   90-36928
                                                          CIP

For David Trethowan Stephens

Contents

List of Figures

List of Tables

Acknowledgements

I am deeply grateful to many people for help in researching and writing the following book. First and foremost I must thank Professor Takamichi Uesugi who not only acted as my host during my two periods as Visiting Scholar at Kyoto University, but also read and commented on the first draft of the manuscript. He was always a most creative adviser, and spent much time showing me the educational institutions of Japan and in academic discussion with me. The failings of the book remain very much mine, but the second draft improvements were the result of his suggestions.

As will be noted in the text, my Japanese friend of longest standing is Professor Masahisa Usui. He was formerly Dean of the Faculty of Education at Toyko University, and will see how our debates over some two decades have influenced my thinking. He also taught many of Japan's most distinguished Professors who, like him, were sources of ideas, information and material for me.

As always, I made unreasonable demands on friends. In particular I would wish to mention Professor Takeshi Ogawa, a singularly generous man, who gave richly of his time, knowledge and material resources. Professor Kazuyo Yamamoto not only introduced me to key personalities and organisations in Japanese education, and spent much time with me, but also taught me about Noh and Kabuki. Professor Sadahiko Fujioka and Professor Shuichi Shimada always provided me with intellectual excitement, good company, and were generous to a fault. Professor Kosack Miyasaka made sure that Tokyo University effectively opened its resources to me, and was ever stimulating in his ideas and originality. Professor Makoto Yamaguchi was a great source of excellent research papers, insights and suggestions, and invigorating company.

Others who were of considerable assistance to me include Professor Hideo Fujita of Rissho University, Hiroko Hashimoto, Head of the Information and International Exchange Division of the National Women's Education Centre, Professor Motoaki Hagiwara of Gumma University, Teruko Ohno (Director) and her team at the Women's Education Division of the Ministry's Life-long Learning Bureau, who could not have been more helpful; similarly Director Hideo Satow and Director Shogo Ichikawa of the National Institute for Educational Research were of great assistance, as was Professor

Shozan Shibano of Kyoto University, and Yoshimori Suzuki of the Education Division of the National Diet Library, who was everything I expect of the best of professionals. My apologies for not listing the many others who made Japan a delight for me to visit.

Finally I must thank a number of postgraduate students who made such stimulating company, led me to laugh a lot, and were full of ideas and kindness. Kenji Miwa of Tokyo University and Yoko Watanabe of Ochanomizu University gave considerably of their time, expertise, and were good company. Similarly Hiromi Murofushi, Takako Maeda, and Naoko Ohta added to my ideas and enjoyable experience. The quality of Japanese postgraduate students should greatly reassure the country.

My fieldwork in Japan would not have been possible without paid leave of absence from my University, and funding from the Japan Society for the Promotion of Science, the Great Britain-Sasakawa Foundation, and the Japan Foundation Endowment Committee. My many thanks!

Michael D. Stephens

1 On Being Japanese

I am bewitched with being British. A Japanese is equally enamoured with being Japanese. Such nationalism can be both creative and destructive. The 1930s and 1940s saw Japan in the grip of a wasteful nationalism, just as Britain has indulged itself on the international football terraces and other violent venues during the 1980s. Even in the 1980s it could lead former Prime Minister Nakasone to make a patently absurd statement that Japan's strength is derived from its homogeneous (that is, pure) population. It is obvious that the Japanese population is a mixture of Asian and South Pacific peoples; there are no 'pure' populations.

In contrast to such flights of self-indulgence Japanese nationalism since 1945 has been a driving power for economic and social recovery. My friend Nagako Sejima, when showing me her ancestral home amidst April's cherry blossoms, spoke of the conditions in Japan in 1945 and 1946. Tokyo and similar urban areas were facing famine. She was in her mid-teens. Her father was an eminent army officer, a samuri demoralised by defeat. To go from people starving to being the richest country on earth in 40 years is a stunning achievement. As in all such human affairs, there is a human cost. Nagako Sejima was of the generation which missed out on such central riches as full secondary and higher education. Japan is less kind than Britain on those seeking a second-chance education. Her efforts since to gain further intellectual development would have impressed Samuel Smiles. To an outsider the system does not seem sympathetic to those who have missed the normal route into higher education. For a woman the challenge appears even greater.

A British academic used to be brought up in the belief that British universities were intellectually superior to those of other countries. It was another example of negative nationalism. Even as a young man I was curious as to how this self-deception could be sustained; after all, the nineteenth century (the British century) saw German universities paramount and imitated almost universally. During this century British universities have been at their most creative, but have had to acknowledge that foreign universities, usually of late American, often had the edge in research excellence. In modern Japanese universities the former British attitude seemingly prevails. 'A Japanese must get a Japanese doctorate if he wishes to be an

1

academic in a Japanese university', confided a postgraduate student at Tokyo University. I feel Mr Nakasone would approve, but such restriction will inhibit the intellectual life of Japanese campuses. Of course, the Japanese try to get the best of both worlds. They practice the nationalism of the PhD, but encourage such students to spend a year abroad. However, it is inadvisable for a young academic to be too 'Westernised'. When the next generation reach their full professorships will they be like-minded? In the sciences Japan is increasingly like Britain or the United States, and relatively young men and women collect their PhDs, but a doctorate in the humanities from Kyoto or Tokyo is still an old man's game.

Although Europeans and Americans are careful to avoid saying it, we live in a Western-created world. The Industrial Revolution transformed how humankind functions, just as the Neolithic Revolution had done previously. The Japanese have entered fully into that world over the last 120 years, as throughout the nineteenth century many of them knew that they would have to. But they have managed to remain uniquely Japanese. In this respect they are very like we British. We have always borrowed other people's good ideas, but remained notable for our Britishness. We created the Industrial Revolution from our borrowings and resulting innovations. The Japanese have often been accused of imitation as if it is some national failing. All dynamic societies emulate in the full knowledge that no single country has a monopoly on excellent practices. A culture is in trouble when its leader, in this instance China's Emperor Chien Lung, can inform the British king via a delegation in 1793 led by Lord Macartney, 'Strange and costly objects do not interest me. As your Ambassador can see for himself we possess all things. I set no value on strange objects and ingeniousness, and have no use for your country's manufactures'. In contrast to this the nationalist Hirata Atsutane in 1811 in his 'Kodo Taii' could state that the 'Japanese should explore all the different kinds of learning despite them being foreign and thus choose the best and put them at the service of the country'. By such similarly timed quotations it becomes easier to understand why Japan is amongst the most highly developed countries and China remains a developing economy. China has paid dearly for its historically induced complacency. Japan's nationalism might suspect the West, but realised it had to borrow from it. As Fukuzawa Yukichi proclaimed in his biographical dictations of 1898, 'The end purpose of all my work was to establish in Japan a civilised country, as well equipped in both the arts of war and peace as nations of the

West'. As we shall see, this victory of Japan's modernisers during the latter part of the nineteenth century had to be achieved against considerable conservative opposition. After all, Japan had closed its ports to most Western contacts from the early seventeenth century to the second half of the nineteenth. But the awesome provincialism of their Chinese neighbours was not to be repeated in Japan. Although modern Japan is often accused of being self-contained this comment comes from Westerners who do not understand the need of an old and rich culture to protect itself from being swamped by the all-powerful Western model. Japan is a totally modern Western economy whilst remaining firmly Japanese in its culture. Its ability to remain very much itself whilst achieving huge economic success should not be a matter of unease to the rest of us.

The cultural differences between the British and Americans or the British and the French are much less than those between the British and the Japanese. It is hoped that this book will indicate some of this variety. There is a tendency in the West to fear the differences, rather than to welcome the resulting richness. This would seem unwise. Where there are differences the Japanese position is always based on logic and, as with all states, the country's historical experience. Of course, I am prejudiced in my views as I have a great liking for the Japanese. I have found them full of humour, generous to a fault, and of overwhelming hospitality. They are usually discreet in their nationalism and sensitive to the feelings of a stranger. When giving a lecture at a Japanese university the foreigner will initially be disconcerted by the silence which greets him at the end of his talk when he invites questions. His audience are seeking questions of a quality which will reflect well on him. It is not enough to ask any old question; the question must flatter the speaker by its distinction. Japanese audiences do ask very good questions.

I was strolling down Higashioji Dori in Kyoto early one afternoon when I passed a baker's shop. A woman buying bread saw me and ran to catch me. I was startled to feel a hand touch my elbow. She was middle aged and modestly dressed. She had no English, but presented me with two beautifully wrapped fruit pies. There was no practical reason for her act of generosity. I had no novelty value as Kyoto is one of the great tourist cities of the world. It was just a demonstration of good-will from one human being to another. Much of this book is about education which the Japanese have made central to their culture and which is without parallel anywhere in the West. The eminent educationalist Yamazaki Ansai stated in his Principles of Education of 1650, 'It would seem to me that the aim of education, elementary and advanced, is to clarify human relationships'. My Kyoto fruit pies, which I ate with particular pleasure as I continued my journey, I consider a demonstration of the extent to which at least one woman had taken to heart her seventeenth-century countryman's teachings. I was the product of a different culture and could only thank her with obvious gratitude and notable surprise. We do not work as hard at clarifying human relationships.

An old friend, when I allow my enthusiasm for Japan to become unBritish, reminds me of the cruelty towards Allied prisoners of the Imperial Army in the Second World War. As in Germany, hyped-up nationalism usually led in Japan to feelings of racial superiority. Such feelings deaden normal sensitivities. If the Japanese record of treatment of prisoners-of-war was dishonourable and beyond excuse its actions in China during the 1930s and 1940s were worse. Whilst I have never believed that the sins of the fathers should be visited upon the sons, there is a danger in brushing aside the memory of such nationalist-inspired madness. The Imperial Rescript to Young People of 22 May 1939 stated, 'The duty of Our subjects to foster national entity, to cultivate national power, and thus eternally to maintain the trend of Our national growth is heavy and its road long. The realisation of these aims is on the shoulders of you students, young in age. We command you to respect valour and virtue, put honour above all things, consider the history of the present and of the past, to clarify your own thinking, deepen and widen your outlook, and never lose sight of balance and the sense of justice in the realisation of your aim; and by fully understanding of your own talent and duty, to cultivate your literary power, learn military discipline, and develop and muster the spirit of fortitude and manliness: thus accomplishing the Great Duty which has been placed upon your shoulders'. Alas, too often crude commitment to country emasculated 'the sense of justice'.

Whilst travelling on a country train which stopped at every small town I had to share a seat with an obviously drunken elderly man who was in high spirits. He was in his best grey suit and still consuming cans of beer. A quieter old man sat opposite him. I asked what was the significance of the badge in his lapel. My question was both an unwise initiative, as he insisted on sharing his cans of beer with me and I finished the trip soaked in the beverage from chest to knees, and a revealing further insight into Japanese history during the 1930s and 1940s. The badge showed that the old man had been wounded. He had been part of the army which took Singapore. On finding that I was British his pleasure was complete. I added further to his enjoyment by revealing that my father had been an air crewman in Burma during the last two years of the war.

Both old men had no rancour towards their former enemies. Their appearance and actions suggested simple countrymen who went to where-so-ever the Emperor commanded them. My new and inebriated friend, who had spent the war as a private, kept the alcohol flowing whilst shouting 'You are an English gentleman!' On my departure he insisted on giving me his name and address. His writing was beautiful and fluent. In the 1930s the Emperor might send his young men to fight in China, but he made sure they had a good grounding in writing and arithmetic first.

The urbanisation of Japan is recent. Even in the early 1950s over 40 per cent of the population were living in the rural areas. The Japanese of today is different from the citizen of the 1930s for he or she is now city-based. The governments of the 1930s could generate their crude nationalism in a less sophisticated, substantially rural population. This is not to ignore the complex debates and varieties of politics which had enriched the Japan of much of the 1920s, but to suggest that there was a large and relatively artless population willing to do their Imperial duty, whatever that might be, waiting in the wings.

The Japanese of the 1930s and 1940s had marched off to their imperial wars in much the same manner as we British did a century earlier. We gave China the burden of the Opium War which had as its overture *HMS Volage* destroying three Chinese junks in August 1839. By the 1930s Japan was pursuing similar ambitions in China, but with the much more destructive technology of the twentieth century. Neither of us came out of China with as much honour as we needed to. At least both of us learned much from the experience. We have all the appearance of being wiser; it is to be hoped that the Chinese will be more enlightened and forgiving than we were.

The Japanese think deeply of their increasingly important international position. Nagako Sejima startled me, as her thoughts often have, by stating, 'Britain dominated the world for a hundred years, America for perhaps 40, but we will be lucky to have 20 years of influence and our economic great power status is already well into those two decades'. So many of the Japanese seem unsure of, and insecure in, their economic success. Perhaps this reflects the times we live in, but I feel this is too trite an explanation. Here are the Japanese demonstrating their economic supremacy, but expecting it to disappear virtually overnight. Perhaps the defeats of the 1940s made them a nation of realists. Or, as the most literate people on earth, they are more aware of the lessons of history than the poorly-read British.

When I visited the giant Matsushita Electric Industrial Company with my old friend Professor Takamichi Uesugi of Kyoto University much of our time with Kakuo Itoh and Tadayoshi Nishioka, the senior staff, was spent in discussing the philosophy of the company's founder Konosuke Matsushita. Such quotations of his as 'this company makes many things and also good men and women', which were used in our discussions led me to read further. In Matsushita's booklet of 1978 entitled 'My Management Philosophy' there are such paragraphs as 'Some people think that the whole purpose of an enterprise is to make a profit. I would agree that profit is indispensable to any enterprise...But while profit is essential, it is not the ultimate goal. The goal must be to improve human life. Profit becomes important and necessary only to the achievement of this goal'. How does a modern monetarist come to terms with Matsushita's statement, 'Enterprises exist as public institutions and are managed in a public context, duty-bound to contribute to the improvement of human life. It is only when they begin to fulfil this duty that their existence begins to have any real meaning'? Mr Itoh informed me that the Company had about 80 000 employees in Japan and 50 000 abroad.

Konosuke Matsushita also wrote, 'The wise man never thinks he knows enough and always seeks out the experience and wisdom of others'. It is little wonder that the Japanese are so obsessed with the importance of education. We lack an economic leadership with the same belief in the centrality of education.

Dr Itsuhiko Sejima, with unfailing generosity, took me on his retirement week-end. I was to be in Tokyo. His colleagues had asked him what they might give him as a retirement present before he left his post as Executive Director of the Japan Electrical Manufacturers' Association. He had requested the trip. I was an unexpected intruder. I could not have been made more welcome. My embarrassment at gate-crashing quickly disappeared.

The group consisted of senior executives from such famous Japanese companies as Toshiba and Hitachi. Almost all were graduates of Tokyo University, although my host's degrees were from Osaka University (another former Imperial institution) and there was one man from Waseda University, perhaps the most famous of the private universities. As we shall see later, prestige institutions in education are the most obvious routes into positions of power within Japan.

Those who go to the right primary schools, high schools and universities end up dominating the economy or leading the government and civil service. There are distinct advantages in getting into a favoured kindergarten in the run up to primary school.

At the dinner for Dr Sejima on the Saturday evening the food and our dress would have put at ease the most traditional of the Japanese. They were as if no Meiji Restoration had taken place in 1868. But the conversation and the style of the evening demonstrated the breadth of knowledge and apt combination of things Japanese and things foreign achieved. The Japanese belief in making education central to everything else has produced businessmen of erudite characteristics. My first conversation at the dinner table (we sat on the floor) was on the novels of Mrs Gaskell. I was struggling to recall the two or three books of hers which I had read in my teens whilst my companion moved easily amongst her writings. Later he explained the evolution of Chinese writing and the changes instituted by the Japanese when they borrowed the script. He was a Tokyo-educated electrical engineer.

The 1872 Code of Education (Gakusei) states in its preamble, 'It is only by building up his character, developing his mind, and cultivating his talents that man may make his way in the world, employ his wealth wisely, make his business prosper, and thus attain the goal of life. But man cannot build up his character, develop his mind, or cultivate his talents without education – that is the reason for establishing schools. Language, writing, and arithmetic, to begin with, are daily necessities in military affairs, government, agriculture, trade, arts, law, politics, astronomy, and medicine. There is not, in short, a single phase of human activity which is not based on learning. Only by striving in the line of his natural aptitude can man prosper in his undertakings, accumulate wealth, and succeed in life. Learning is the key to success in life, and no man can afford to neglect it. It is ignorance that leads man astray, makes him destitute, disrupts his family, and in the end destroys his life'.

The results of such a national commitment were there for me to study during Dr Sejima's retirement trip. All the Japanese executives could speak English, although with varying degrees of fluency. Much to my discomfort during our Saturday evening they displayed a remarkable memory for English and Scottish folk-songs and for English poetry. When called upon to sing an English song all that came to my desperate mind were the words of 'Dashing Away With a Smoothing Iron'. My voice is tuneless. Such was my contribution to the 'retirement' melodies. Despite such an unimpressive effort I was loudly clapped and cheered. At the end of the evening I was able to show some leadership qualities in the organising of a rendition by all present of Auld Lang Syne. The weekend showed me to be a product of Western civilisation, whilst my Japanese colleagues apparently flowed effortlessly between the cultures of Europe and Japan. They also showed impressive social skills. Whilst the central reason for the trip was never lost sight of, namely Dr Sejima's retirement, I was integrated into the group. I found it impossible to pay for anything, and was rarely left without company. If, as is frequently proclaimed, the Japanese give priority to the group and not the individual this is not necessarily oppressive to the individual.

On the Bullet Train from Kyoto to Tokyo the man in the seat next to me gave all the signs that he was preparing to speak to me. It took him several minutes before he opened a conversation. I was so fascinated by the signals he gave out of his intention that I did not short-circuit the process by speaking first. I was impressed by his courage in beginning something in a foreign language with a stranger. He made a most pleasant companion amidst the luxury of Japan's superb train. His name was Kiyoshi Kawakubo and he owned Osaka Books Limited. Once again I found myself discussing English literature. Amidst the dust and dirt of British Rail do Japanese visitors find themselves talking to the British about the modern Japanese novel or Japanese poetry? Perhaps.

Before we parted at Tokyo Kiyoshi Kawakubo gave me a copy of James Berry's 'Chain of Days'. He had greatly enjoyed the poems it contained. I have read them with pleasure since. Another totally unexpected gift from a man of rich learning.

My Japanese friend of longest standing is Masa Usui. When I was in charge of a small unit at Liverpool University he came to spend a year with us at the beginning of the 1970s. He was already a professor at Tokyo University. He proved to be a man of impeccable manners with a delicious sense of humour. During what must have been a strange and difficult time for him we saw only his charm and even temper. It was then that I recognised one of the great challenges in life. Is it possible to give a Japanese as many presents as he will lavish on you? For 18 years I have tried to show my high regard for Masa Usui by giving him surprise gifts, but he always returns presents in greater profusion.

In 1904 Lafcadio Hearn, who became a Japanese citizen, wrote of his adopted country, 'The whole nation is being educated, with

Government help, upon a European plan; and the full programme includes the chief subjects of Western study. From kindergarten to university the entire system is modern in outward seeming; yet the effect of the new education is much less marked in thought and sentiment than might be supposed'. Masa Usui has taken what he needs from Western knowledge, but follows the traditions of Japanese good manners. I shall never manage to have him obligated to me in the matter of gifts. At our last meeting he gave me two of the sake cups he had as a youth at the most famous high school of pre-1945 Japan. I am outclassed. A Japanese will give what he himself has used as a sign of warm friendship.

The United States Department of State issued Directive 74 on the revision of the Japanese Educational System on 27 March 1947. For a Western audience it is an attractive document, but many of its assumptions went against Japanese tradition. It begins, 'Education should be looked upon as the pursuit of truth, as a preparation for life in a democratic nation, and as a training for the social and political responsibilities which freedom entails. Emphasis should be placed on the dignity and worth of the individual, on independent thought and initiative, and on developing a spirit of inquiry. The interdependent character of international life should be stressed. The spirit of justice, fair play, and respect for the rights of others, particularly minorities, and the necessity of friendship based upon mutual respect for people of all races and religions, should be emphasised. Special emphasis should also be placed on the teaching of the sanctity of the pledged word in all human relations, whether between individuals or nations. Measures should be taken as rapidly as possible to achieve equality of educational opportunity for all regardless of sex or social position. The revision of the Japanese educational system should, in large measure, be undertaken by the Japanese themselves . . . ' The Japanese have been selective in which of these exhortations they accept. It is a much less class-ridden country than Britain, for example, but, as noted earlier, the cult of the individual which is one of the strengths (and weaknesses) of the West has not yet challenged the commitment to the group. A trip to the Osaka Human Rights Museum would show how seriously the Japanese are trying to integrate their former outcast burakumin ('special village people') and to act decently towards such long-established immigrant groups as the Koreans. But it always seems difficult for the Japanese to accept those who do not fully conform. To be different, unlike the much proclaimed British cult of the admired eccentric, costs you dear in Japan. Japanese professors have Japanese PhDs. Japan sees itself as unique and its citizens must conform to that uniqueness. Most countries recognise their uniqueness, but in Japan it is an excluding factor. It will be most interesting to see how the imminent huge immigration which Japan's fabled prosperity will induce will be handled. Will Japan be able to accept more of the attitudes displayed by America, that country of immigrants? As Japan has noted that it cannot stop the arrival of immigrants, which will often be by illegal entry, will it change the meaning of nihonjinron (on being Japanese)?

All countries are to some extent corrupt. The issue is whether the degree of corruption is debilitating to that society or not. By international standards corruption in Japan is modest. Whilst it is less crime-stricken by far than America, it is no more open and democratic in its government than Britain. It is a well-ordered country with an inadequate road system.

The Imperial Rescript of 1879 on the Great Principles of Education stated, 'The essence of education, our traditional national aim, and a watchword for all men, is to make clear the ways of benevolence, justice, loyalty, and filial piety, and to master knowledge and skill and through these to pursue the Way of Man. In recent days, people have been going to extremes. They take unto themselves a foreign civilisation whose only values are fact-gathering and technique, thus violating the rules of good manners and bringing harm to our customary ways. Although we set out to take in the best features of the West and bring in new things in order to achieve the high aims of the Meiji Restoration – abandonment of the undesirable practices of the past and learning from the outside world – this procedure had a serious defect. It reduced benevolence, justice, loyalty, and filial piety to a secondary position. The danger of indiscriminate emulation of Western ways is that in the end our people will forget the great principles governing the relations between ruler and subject, and father and son. Our aim, based on our ancestral teachings, is solely the clarification of benevolence, justice, loyalty, and filial piety'. A good case could be made out to suggest that this conservative document established many of the foundations of modern Japan. The attitudes inherited from the feudal Japan of the previous Tokugawa regime remain deeply influential into the 1980s. Whilst this often makes Japan less corrupt than the United States it also produces very differing attitudes. The Japanese worship at the shrine of harmony. Their culture revolves around an obsessive need to achieve group unity. This need not be undemocratic as the group will adjust its posture to accommodate nuances within its members' attitudes. But in the end the group must achieve harmony. Similarly, the need of feudal Japan to encourage hard-work to survive in a physical environment much harsher than that of Britain continues with workers seeing long hours and high commitment as a moral good and a cause for individual and group satisfaction. These Japanese differences are of great complexity and we in the West too often interpret them in a simple-minded and condescending manner. Interdependence in Japanese society is seen as a rich support of the individual, not necessarily as a stifling of the personality.

All schools reflect the society of which they are a critical part. Although Japan has achieved a certain notoriety because of its much publicised 'examination hell' the education system welcomes the new pupils as if all Japanese citizens are of equal talent and ability. The schools' ideology is of likeness amongst its charges and of egalitarian treatment. In a population which takes education so seriously this is a positive contribution. All pupils and students are valued. All parents, and especially mothers, are expected to work with their children to help them in their learning. A failure to reach an agreed educational objective is as much a defeat for the teacher and the mother as for the child. Usually such shared responsibility leaves the pupil less scarred than in British schools. The school year contains substantially more hours than does its British equivalent, and by the time junior high school arrives most Japanese will be attending a crammer (juku) after normal school hours, but such hard work fits in with the mainstream culture and appears not to be resented by the pupil. As we shall see, the Japanese education system, whilst acknowledging the innovative contribution of the Americans after 1945, pre-dates in its major characteristics the drive for modernisation after 1868. It could be suggested that it is more in tune with Japanese society at this point in time than is the British educational system with British society. Whether this will remain so might be questioned. Of all the developed countries Japan will face the greatest social changes over the next 50 years.

Professor Miyasaka of Tokyo University spent an academic year with us in Nottingham. For a Western scholar this would not be unusual, but I remain impressed by Professor Miyasaka's initiative, as with his mentor Professor Usui's similar stay in Liverpool. Except for a brief visit to South Korea he had not been abroad before. In middle age he left his family to spend many months 9000 miles from home in a most alien culture. The Japanese take on a job with total commitment. In the second term Professor Miyasaka asked if he might speak to one of my postgraduate classes. We had been dealing with the history of British adult education. Over the next 45 minutes he displayed great learning and many fresh insights into the subject. It was an intellectual tour de force. Those who believe that the Japanese education system crushes intellectual originality have not heard my friends Professors Usui, Uesugi, Miyasaka, and Shimada give papers. Over the next decades the Japanese will become an increasing intellectual force in the world. As Britain spends relatively less on its universities, so we shall see ourselves replaced by the high investment Japanese. It is worth repeating endlessly that the Japanese treat education much more seriously than do we British. Such being the case, they have a better educated population than we do and the gap between us is increasing. It is only a matter of time before the American domination of the Nobel prizes is challenged by Japan. Professor Fujioka and Professor Shimada are great singers of Scottish folk-songs. Sadahiko Fujioka spent a year at Sheffield University and Shuichi Shimada at Nottingham. They are noted radicals within Japanese social education circles. Their writings and field involvement are rightly well known. On my first day in Tokyo I was their guest at the most expensive hotel in that most expensive of cities. There was superb food and they wished to welcome me to their home patch with a magnificent view of the imperial palace. We sat chatting with the latter set-out before us. Despite their radicalism they were there to enjoy a truly capitalist environment. They were comfortable, full of wit and charm, and determined to spoil me. They made their wives laugh continuously and talked to the head waiter as if they had come twice daily for the previous ten years. A British radical probably would not have been so relaxed in such an environment. The occasion was an accolade to the Minister of Education Oki Takato's instruction 'Explanation of School Matters' of 17 November 1891, 'If the aim of regular education is to make known the proper relations between man and man, to make the Japanese people understand their proper role, and to raise the quality and welfare of society and nation, every person who lives in this country must receive a regular education . . . . . Rather than provide perfect facilities for a limited number of children, our policy must be to provide compulsory education for the largest number'. By providing well for all children Japan has created a citizenry which suffers less from class discomfort than in most Western countries. A radical may enjoy the good things in the capitalist's world, and still believe in a different tomorrow.

Professor Kazuyo Yamamoto reminded me of just how good many Japanese are at relations between human beings. Amongst a thousand kindnesses she provided during a stay in Tokyo I recall her regal arrival on the Tokyo railway station platform to see me off. Kenji Miwa had helped me with my luggage from Tokyo University and found my seat. Professor Yamamoto appeared five minutes before the train was due to leave, as with most Japanese women superbly attired, and presented me with that morning's edition of *The Japan Times*, a beautiful luncheon basket and cool drinks. Efficient, well-timed, and thoughtful.

Although the PhD students Kenji Miwa of Tokyo University and Yoko Watanabe of Ochanomizu University during the same stay in Tokyo had given up much of their time to look after me, such generosity of spirit may be a dying Japanese tradition. Relations between human beings may be a waning priority. Many graduate students when now asked to help entertain visitors will tell their professors they do not have the time. What they are disguising by such a lame excuse is the familiar Western question, 'What is in it for me?' Looking after a professor from England does not give the immediate return that some juku teaching provides. Are we into the next stage of Japanese social change?

2 The View From 1876

In education, which demands ideals, it is often hard to hang onto one's idealism. This is particularly true in England where education has usually been a frail plant reluctantly given water and nutrients by the state. Ever since the nineteenth century the London Government's cry has been one of 'Value for Money!' which really means 'How Little Dare We Spend on Education?' In the nineteenth century Britain was the richest country on earth and Robert Lowe, Vice-President of the Department of Education, when introducing his Revised Code of Regulations of 1861, caught the traditional English mood on education by stating to the House of Commons, 'If this system is not cheap, I can promise it shall be efficient; if it is not efficient, it shall be cheap'. The resulting 'payment-by-results', as has often been the English experience, was neither.

By British standards nineteenth-century Japan was a poor country. However, it saw educational investment as central to its development. Its plans and ambitions, as we shall see, could not be matched by state funding during the early decades of reform following the Meiji Restoration of 1868. But its ambitions were impressive and eventually realised in the twentieth century. This chapter explores the Japanese attitudes to education immediately after the Restoration. Most of the information comes from a document prepared by the newly established Japanese Department of Education for the 1876 Philadelphia International Exhibition under the title of 'Outline History of Japanese Education'. It is 202 pages long and has seven chapters. The introductory chapter was prepared by the Foreign Superintendent of Education in Japan, David Murray, who came as adviser to Tanaka Fujimaro in 1873 and left in 1878 when the conservative reaction saw his patron falling into disfavour. Murray had been on the staff of Rutgers University. Mori Arinori had arrived as Japan's first Chargé d'Affaires to the United States in 1872 and had then written to various eminent Americans asking their views on the development of Japanese education. Mori had been much taken by Professor Murray's reply. Chapter 1 (General Sketch), Chapter 2 (Education in the Early Ages), Chapter 3 (Education Under the Shogunate), and Chapter 4 (Education Since the Revolution) were put together by Otzuki Sinji and Naka Michitaka. Chapter 5

14

(Japanese Language and Learning) and Chapter 6 (Japanese Arts and Sciences) were the work of Sakakibara Yosino. What the book suggests powerfully is that Japan had a long and substantial educational history which provided a wide-ranging foundation for Western developments. Japan after 1868 was more like a Second World country developing towards the First World, rather than as it is normally depicted, a Third World country.

As I watched members of Japan's glitterati at a preview of an exhibition of sixteenth and seventeenth-century Japanese objects d'art in the commercial and industrial heartland of Osaka I was reminded of part of David Murray's letter of 7 March 1872 in reply to Mori Arinori's enquiry, 'Education does three things which bear upon the material prosperity of a country:

1. It stimulates in the mind of the individual a desire to improve his present condition, and aids him in devising ways and means.
2. It teaches what has been done in other lands, and by other men in like pursuits.
3. It opens up to him the principles which underlie his vocation, and gives him a sure scientific basis for his future efforts.'

The Japanese took to heart many of the teachings of the Westerners they employed or whose advice they had sought, but notably when it coincided with their own traditions and experience. My enjoyment of the Osaka exhibition resulted from the generosity and company of my host Professor Uesugi, the technical brilliance of Japanese artistic achievement some centuries earlier, and the style and affluence of the largely female audience. Japan has come a long way since 1868, or has it?

In 1876 Otzuki Sinji told the world that books came to Japan via Korea in 200 AD and that the first use of writing for public affairs was in the reign of the Emperor Richu at the beginning of the fifth century AD. In 507 AD the Emperor Keitai invited Korean professors to teach the Chinese classics. During the reign of the Empress Suiko at the end of the sixth century an ambassador was sent to the Chinese court. The Japanese Takamuku Kuromasa and Bin were educated in China and returned in 645 to help in the government of the Emperor Kotoku. In 668 the Emperor Tenji took the first steps to establish an educational institution with a number of professors appointed. In 702 the Emperor Taiho reorganised the university and established schools in each province. Students were to study for nine years with a view to becoming civil servants. Later in the century the practice of rewarding men of learning was established. Courses included the six Chinese classics, history, composition, law, mathematics, and penmanship. There were also courses in medicine, astronomy, and astrology. By the eighth century students were recruited from certain hereditary families.

What these descriptions of early Japanese educational history illustrate in the writings of 1876 is contemporary belief that Japan had a long and honourable record with which to bolster its self-confidence when facing the onslaught of Western ideas and technology. It also demonstrated that earlier it had faced a similar situation with the impact of Chinese and, notably, Korean culture. From the invasion of a thousand or more years before it had gained great benefit whilst remaining true to itself. The writer is also keen to show that education and its attendant institutions had been highly regarded by previous generations when facing cultural imperialism from abroad. In a world where it was necessary to implement the old adage 'if you can't beat them then join them' the Japanese had to recognise education as the necessary vehicle.

Otzuki Sinji piled historical fact upon historical fact in order to establish the authority for seeing education as an ancient pursuit in Japan. In the later eighth century Isonokami Iyetsugu is listed as establishing a public library in the new centre of power of Kyoto, with Wage Hiroyo and Sugawara Michizane doing the same a little later. Similarly, 'Fujiwara Yorinanga, a minister of state, who was very fond of literary pursuits, purchased a great number of books, which he arranged in the four classes of Chinese classics, histories, miscellaneous, and Japanese books, and placed them on shelves, distinguished from one another. The greater part of the books were of his own copying'.

We learn that the first history of Japan ('Nihonshoki') was completed in 720, and this was followed by further histories which are defiantly described, 'All these are authentic histories of this country'. Suitable quotations are provided to reinforce the impression of the Japanese having always regarded education as of central importance, such as that of Miyoshi Kiyotsura in 914: 'The successful government of a country depends upon wisdom, and wisdom depends upon education'. The sentence comes from a request to the Emperor to increase the funding for education. The next pages are full of details of schools established and libraries founded in the following centuries, plus such information as, 'Printing was first used as early as in the reign of the Empress Koken (749), when 'Mukuseijokio', a sacred book of the Buddhists, was printed; but since that time no mention is made of printing books for the space of nearly four hundred years, till the third year of Shoan (1301) when 'Gokenho' was printed'. Then, with some eccentricity, Otzuki Sinji continues, '"Hanniyakio", a sacred book of the Buddhists, was printed in the first year of Genriyaku (1184) . . . '

Professor Takamichi Uesugi has three delightful, contrasting and lively daughters called Tomoko, Yoriko, and Nobuko, and they are now young women who have either graduated from university or are studying there. When first I met them during their father's academic year in Britain their charm instantly brought to mind Gilbert and Sullivan's 'Three Little Girls From School Are We'. They are privileged in having Takamichi and Mitsuyo Uesugi as their parents, for higher education is an expensive business in Japan. As in most countries, and we shall explore this in greater detail later, women in Japan have yet to achieve equality in many areas of life. Of the 1985 university entrants 307 960 were male and 104 033 female. In contrast 157 826 women attended the two-year junior colleges as against 15 677 men.

I use these statistics at this point to illustrate the ground yet to be covered in achieving equality of the sexes in education, but also to remind the reader of what progress has been made since 1868. Such documents as the 1876 Japanese Department of Education book for Philadelphia ensured that education came top of the list of national priorities. It high-jacked Japanese history, always a fuel for nationalism, to promote education as a national obsession. Although there is always a time-lag between provision for males and the equally important recognition of women's education if the Japanese were to be conditioned into seeing education as all-important inevitably there would be a realisation that the whole population would need to be provided for.

Those pushing the case for education in the key years following the Meiji Restoration were highly selective in their use of historical evidence. For example, they tended to ignore a key document like Kaibara Ekken's 'The Greater Learning for Women' of 1672. It includes such harsh definitions as, 'The only qualities that befit a woman are gentle obedience, chastity, mercy, and quietness', and frequently states, 'the great lifelong duty of a woman is obedience'. The author felt that, 'The five worst maladies that afflict the female mind are: indocility, discontent, slander, jealousy, and silliness.

Without any doubt, these five maladies infest seven or eight out of every ten women, and it is from these that arises the inferiority of women to men'. Finally, the apparently happily married Kaibara Ekken could muse, 'Such is the stupidity of her character that it is incumbent on her, in every particular, to distrust herself and to obey her husband'. Whilst the builders of the new Japan in the nineteenth century could establish the over-riding importance of education, gaining equality for women within provision had much tradition to bury.

The last two pages of Otzuki Sinji's Chapter 1 begin with the list of schools established during the seventeenth century when Kaibara Ekken was setting such harsh limits to the lives of women. The author quickly brings the reader from the Tokugawa Period to the Meiji Era when (1872) the Japanese Department of Education was first established.

The book's Chapter 2 is entitled 'Education in the Early Ages', and begins, 'The education of the people being the foundation of good government, it has never been neglected by those who have aimed at promoting the prosperity of a country, and the happiness of its people. To furnish, therefore, the means of education to every youth in the country, by providing schools and teachers of various branches of knowledge, forms one of the most important and necessary measures to be adopted by the state'. This is followed by a paragraph reminding the reader that the use of characters was not known 'till intercourse with foreign countries was opened' (beginning with a visit in 157 BC by a Korean). The interchange between Korea and Japan over the following seven hundred years is then briefly described. From this the reader learns that, for example, a policy was established in 514 AD of inviting Korean professors to come to Japan to teach literature, and that in 528 AD the custom of recruiting students from this educational system to run the imperial civil service was instituted. However, later in the sixth century Buddhism was introduced and many of the educational posts were taken over from the Korean professors by priests.

The author is careful to drive home both the advantages and dangers of foreign intercourse, 'Laws being the only effectual means of suppressing crimes and preventing wrongs, are most important provisions for the preservation of peace and order in a country. But in those early times, when people were, notwithstanding a few instances of revolt, so simple and honest that the state of society approximated to that golden age in which general peace and harmony prevailed without any provision to control their action, there existed nothing like distinctly enacted laws. But, in the offices and prayers of religion, there existed petitions which recognised their sins against Heaven and also crimes against their fellow-men, and the ceremonies for their expiation. But when intercourse with foreigners commenced, and the intelligence of the people was consequently more developed, their habits and manners became to some degree also corrupted. Hence, in the twelfth year of the reign of the Empress Suiko (604 AD), the Prince Shotoku published 17 edicts as the laws of the country'.

By the eighth century there were schools in the capital and the provinces, all of which were to provide during their nine-year curriculum graduates for imperial service. The curriculum and examinations were deeply influenced by Chinese models. 'The candidates for examination for public service were divided into six classes, according to the branch of study in which they had chiefly engaged, viz: first, those who had displayed great talents; second, those who had studied not less than two Chinese classics; third, those who had studied political science, and had also learned to read the imperial annals of China and the selections of Chinese literature; fourth, students of law; fifth, students of penmanship, and, sixth, those in mathematics'. In 782 the tradition of allowances to support full time study for students was introduced. Students were also sent regularly to study in China, beginning in the reign of the Empress Suiko (593-628). Again, this information helped the author to show how long established was overseas inquiry. Otzuki Sinji was writing when there were still at least three major warring ideological factions on such matters. There remained a powerful group who would prefer no contact with the West. There was, in contrast, an increasing faction which was pro-Western and bewitched with Western ideas. Finally there was a party which wanted to use Western knowledge to give Japan economic and military strength to resist the West. Sakuma Shozan (1811–64) typified the latter with his well known phrase 'Western Science, Eastern Morals'.

Chapter 3 ('Education Under the Shogunate') is a revealing essay on the educational foundations of modern Japan laid during the Tokugawa period. As with the previous chapter, it begins with a statement to promote the interests of education, 'By the rigour of military discipline disorder in a country is suppressed, but peace is not preserved without literary knowledge'. Again Otzuki Sinji gives much space to describing the establishing of particular schools and similar institutions, but also tries to keep sight of the broader sweep of history, 'Following this was a period when the imperial power was usurped by the military subjects, for several hundred years, and the educational system could not be kept in so flourishing a condition as in former times, and it was not until the time when Tokugawa Ieyasu rose into power as shogun, or military chief under the emperor, that scholars were esteemed, Confucianism respected, the art of government studied, and the benefit of education began to spread itself once more over the empire'. The Shogunate began in 1603 and was to last until 1867. Tokugawa Ieyasu and his heirs had one major priority, which was to secure their power base. This led in 1636-38 to an elimination of the one potential rival in military strength with the outlawing of seafaring and shipbuilding. There were to be no Japanese seagoing vessels, seamen were to keep to coastal waters, and Japan was closed to most of the outside world. With this went a tense and contrasting cultural explosion. In 1615 an edict defined Bushido, the ethics of the warrior or samurai. Such stylised pursuits for the samurai as the tea ceremony and Noh drama were developed. Often to the discomfort of the Tokugawa regime and the seduction of its samurai the more affluent townspeople supported professional entertainers and artists such as Kabuki actors, geisha girls, and poets and dramatists enjoying urban luxury and license. This creativity was to catch the imagination of nineteenth-century Europe and deeply influence its art.

The Tokugawa from the beginning of their domination of Japan stated that an unlettered samurai was not acceptable. Education based on a Confucian model was to be pursued. In 1630 they established the Shoheiko, a Confucian College, under the principalship of the Hayashi family. Such schools quickly followed for samurai in other parts of Japan. Herbert Passin (*Society and Education in Japan*, Kodansha, Tokyo, 1987, pp.14-15) concludes, 'Educational institutions, and with them literacy, expanded slowly throughout the nineteenth century. But from the end of the eighteenth century growth was rapid in all types of schools in Japan. Between 1781 and 1871, perhaps 200 domain schools were established. Commoner education started later but snowballed even more spectacularly. Of the 416 gogaku (local schools) for commoners in 1872, 7 had been established before 1789, 104 between 1789 and 1867, and 305 in the five years before the establishment of the modern school system. Of the lower-level commoners' schools, the terakoya, 558 were established before 1803; then between 1803 and 1843, another 3,050;

and between 1844 and 1867, 6,691 more'.

Of the Kioho period (1716–35) Otzuki Sinji states, 'there was not a province in which learning was not cultivated, nor a family in which books were not read'. Although the Portuguese had been expelled from Japan in 1639, the Dutch were permitted to remain in Nagasaki from 1641 onwards. The Dutch made an annual visit to the Shogun which saw a number of Japanese learning the Dutch language to act as interpreters, but they were not allowed to read Dutch books or other printed matter. However, during the Kioho period permission was at length granted for some interpreters to read and write Dutch. A number of interested Japanese over the following decades worked on texts in Dutch to master the grammar and vocabulary to gain access to Western knowledge. Events gave further impetus to such initiatives: 'In the fourth year of Bunkwa [1807] difficulties with the Russians took place in the northern parts of the empire. In the following year the appearance of the English on the western coast caused considerable commotion. The Shogun's government decided, therefore, to make itself acquainted with the condition of these two countries, and Moshitsu received orders to compile an account of these countries from the Dutch books. Accordingly, he composed the works in regard to the Russian questions. In the eighth year the shogun's government paid Moshitsu twenty ingots of silver, and continued this payment yearly, making him translator of Dutch works. In the fifth year of Bunsei [1822] he at length received a monthly salary. The above was the first instance of the shogun's government directly encouraging Western learning'.

Moshitsu died in 1827, but the shogun's government continued to employ his son Genkan, who published the first book solely devoted to Dutch grammar. Others were also busy translating Dutch works, such as Awoki Rinso and his disciple Kawamoto Komin in physics, Genshin in medicine, and his son Yo-an the first book on chemistry. Genshin's student, Mitsukuri Gempo, translated works on geography and history. These translations inspired the creation of Western-style institutions such as Yedo's Western Medical Science School established in the Tempo period (1830–43). In 1858 the Shogun appointed doctors of the European school as court physicians. The running costs of the School were taken over by the government and in 1861 it was renamed the European Medical School. The following year a chemistry department was added. In 1861 also a medical school was opened at Nagasaki where it was possible to use Dutch instructors. In 1865 a Dutch academic was employed to teach physics and chemistry at the Nagasaki school. Two years earlier in Nagasaki a foreign languages school began to instruct in Chinese, Dutch, English, French and Russian. The Shogun's government also created a medical school in Osaka.

Amidst all the fine detail of the chapter are frequent insights as to how the author viewed Japan's past and its lessons for his own time. Whilst we are aware of the highly cultivated merchant class which was of singular importance to the development of Japan's rich urban arts of the Tokugawa ascendency, Otzuki Sinji stated, 'The inhabitants of Osaka being principally devoted to commercial pursuits, learning was not thought of much account by them'. There was a need to show something of educational development during the time of the shogunate whilst not being lavish in praise of a system replaced. The chapter is summarised, 'The above is an account of the schools established by the feudal lords after the ascendency of the Tokugawa dynasty; but as yet there were few private schools that had attained any celebrity, although learned men had devoted themselves to teaching scholars collected around them, and had opened boarding-schools, where literature and penmanship were taught. Although private schools did not flourish, we must bear in mind that they lacked the encouragement and support of local government'.

Otzuki Sinji's final contribution (Chapter 4) on the provision of education since the Shogun Tokugawa Keiki resigned in October 1867, is a celebration of momentous events. In 1869 the capital was moved from Kyoto to Yedo, which was renamed Tokyo. The key educational institutions of the latter were placed under government control and new institutions founded such as a college of chemistry and physics in Osaka and a military academy in Kyoto. In 1868 the creation of a school of Japanese learning in Kyoto does much to reveal the state of mind of many of those promoting change in Japan: '1. It is incumbent on every citizen to understand the nature of the public institutions of his country, and to become familiar with the duties pertaining to his position in society. 2. Foreign learning, both Chinese and European, must be made to subserve the interests of Japan. The past calamities of the empire have been due to the usurpation of power and the neglect of their appropriate duties on the part of the military chiefs. Hereafter let all adhere strictly and honestly to the duties belonging to their respective stations. 3. Useless styles of composition, and aimless discourses and discussions, ought to be abandoned in the future methods of education; and the literary and military branches of learning ought to be so cultivated as to be mutually helpful. 4. Japanese and Chinese learning are not antagonistic, and therefore the students of these systems, forgetting their former conflicts, should show forbearance towards each other'.

At the beginning of 1869 the restrictions relating to social rank regarding entrance to certain colleges were removed. This was followed by the Government permitting newspapers to be published. From this time on various changes were made within the Japanese educational system which was expected to promote the 'three natural relations' (between master and servant, father and son, and husband and wife) and the 'Five cardinal virtues' (humanity, uprightness, propriety, wisdom, and sincerity). By 1871 the Government was ready to send a delegation abroad to Europe and America led by Iwakura. Tanaka Fujimaro went as special commissioner for education. The great code of education was published in the second half of 1872. It aimed at providing a national school system with the country divided into eight university districts, which were further subdivided into 32 middle school districts. Each middle school district was to have 210 primary school districts. The aim was to build 54 760 primary schools, but with minimal aid from the national government. The code had to be replaced before the decade was out, but its introductory passages remained of deep influence. Otzuki Sinji quotes extensively from the document, perhaps the key phrase being, 'Learning is no longer to be considered as belonging to the upper classes, but is to be equally the inheritance of nobles and gentry, farmers and artisans, males and females'. The plan may have been made more modest almost as soon as it was published, but the educational vision remained unchanged.

In 1872 the Department of Education opened the Tokyo Public Library. Initially it contained only Japanese and Chinese works, but in 1875 foreign books were included. From the beginning the public could borrow books without charge. The Department also began a rapid expansion of teacher training colleges as a chronic shortage of competent personnel in the elementary schools made itself apparent. In presenting to the Emperor the first Report of the Department of Education in 1875 Tanaka Fujimaro is modest in his claims and cautious about the future, stating, 'But, in regard to its educational duties, it is the humble opinion of your servant that it has in some degree established order and system'. He concludes, 'It is the opinion of your humble servant that the time when complete and correct reports may be obtained, and when such reports shall show that every family is educated and every individual is in good health, can only be reached by gradual and slow approximations'. Otzuki Sinji finishes his four chapters by proclaiming that, 'The most important event in educational matters of the year 1875 was the establishment of a female normal school. It is designed to train female teachers especially for the work of teaching in the elementary schools'. It is of significance that he highlights this piece of female emancipation.

The following two chapters by Sakakibara Yosino are, again, rich in information giving, but also revealing about Japanese views of themselves in 1876. Chapter 5 on Japanese Language and Learning begins with a refuting of Japanese efforts to suggest writing was known in 'the remotest times'. Sakakibara Yosino reminds his readers that the first account of Confucian books being introduced into Japan was in 284 AD when the Korean Ajiki came to teach the Crown Prince Uji Wakairatsuko. There then follows several pages of technical detail on the early Japanese written language and the various influences upon it which came from abroad, 'From about 900 AD students ceased to go to China to study, and, communication with that country becoming infrequent, Chinese grammar became corrupted, and the result was that a hybrid style of composition was created by this confusion. This is the style now used by the Government in its documents, and by people in their daily correspondence'. The substantial literary traditions of Japan are illustrated by a number of pages on poetry, which is divided into six periods: Josei (ancient), Chiuko (early medieval), Nakagoro (medieval), Kinko (later medieval), Kinsei (modern), and Konsei (contemporary).

Japan as an ancient and distinguished civilisation is confirmed by Sakakibara Yosino pointing out that local records offices were created in 403 AD. There followed a custom of history writing which enriched both Buddhism and Shintoism. A thousand years later a revival in Japanese learning amongst priests saw great interest in the writings of the earlier period. As early as 664 AD the Emperor Tenji appointed a Director of Schools. By 676 a university is recorded with 400 students. 'Contemporaneously with the university at Kyoto, schools existed and flourished in all provinces. In each of these provincial schools there was a hakase (professor), a doctor (that is, a medical professor) and so on. In the very large provinces the number of students was 50; in the larger provinces it was 40; in those of medium size it was 30; and in the smaller 20. Those among these students who successfully passed the examinations of the Shikibu (Board of Rites) were admitted to the university. Although it is impossible to say when these provincial schools ceased to exist, yet, owing to the gradual breaking up of the local governments, and to the cessation of the old rule of sending chief magistrates from Kyoto, the diffusion of education came to a standstill in every part of the empire'. The university was in notable decline before the Genkiyo period (1321–23).

Chapter 5 concludes with a discussion of the Japanese examination system. Chapter 6 opens with the statement, 'Although Japanese pictures are not imitations of those of other countries, still the art was originally acquired from foreigners'. Again, we see the simple lesson stressed of a long established part of Japanese culture (it is suggested that painting was first introduced in the fifth century AD from Korea) which originally came from abroad, but which had been made distinctively Japanese. There follows much detail of artists and their work over the period from the fifth to the nineteenth century.

The next section of the final chapter again takes up the theme of the borrowings from abroad in ancient times. In dealing with medicine the author points out that Japan was once more indebted to Korea (during the reign of Emperor Inkiyo 412-453 AD), but continues, 'After this, the Chinese medical system gradually came into use; students went abroad and acquired the arts of surgery, acupuncture, amma (that is, dry shampooing of the body to promote a freer circulation of the blood) and the like. At the same time numerous medical practitioners came over to this country, and the healing art was practised according to Chinese medical works'. As in dealing with the history of painting in Japan, Sakakibara Yosino lists the major figures in medicine and the changing fortunes of native and Chinese imported ideas. In the eighteenth century via the Dutch the Japanese began to take an interest in European medicine, having borrowed ideas on surgery from the Portuguese as early as the beginning of the seventeenth century.

The Chinese and Europeans also feature substantially in the history of what the author calls 'Calendrography'. Chinese ideas on almanacs came via Korea in the sixth century. The Italian Matteo's introduction of automatic striking time-keepers to Ming China saw this technical advance reach Japan at the beginning of the seventeenth century.

To re-establish the authority of Japan as an independently creative country Sakakibara Yosino next describes the ancient art of Japanese papermaking in some detail over five or so pages. Then follows sections on the Japanese pencil or writing-brush, the inkstone, Japanese ink, and the chapter concludes rather abruptly with a paragraph on the engraving of books.

The Japanese Department of Education's substantial document for the 1876 Philadelphia International Exhibition also contains a number of Appendices. Firstly there is the 'Constitution of the Mombusho, or Japanese Department of Education', which covers the staff and regulations. Part II of the Appendices is a 'Chronicle of Events in the Recent History of the Department of Education' and makes an effective eight-page summary of the period from the Meiji Restoration to 1875. Appendix III gives the emperors from Jimmu in 660 BC, whilst this is followed by a list of year periods which line up Japanese dating with Western. Finally there is an Appendix giving a 'Catalogue of Articles Exhibited by the Japanese Department of Education at the International Exhibition, 1876'. This is extensive and ranges from contemporary school equipment to historical material.

The reader's impression after studying the 1876 document is one of a politically aware leadership sharpening, despite continuing debate within Japan, educational objectives to ensure that the Western powers' economic domination was modified. The Japanese were very aware that if they did not become 'modern' they would face the likelihood of being absorbed into the ranks of colonial possessions. As Germany before them, the Japanese were quick to appreciate that the only way to catch up with the economic superpower Britain was through education. The Japanese began their modernisation by placing educational investment centre-stage, although initially they expected much of the resourcing to come from local sources over time. This paid off supremely well, as it did also in Germany. It is a lesson, as we shall see, never forgotten whatever the political environment within Japan. Of all the peoples on earth the Japanese seem the most convinced of the importance of education and are willing to make a high personal investment in it at all levels of society.

Such cultural attitudes would appear to have much to do with Japan's economic success.

A second point arising from the 1876 document needs further stressing, although previously mentioned. Judging by the standards of the second half of the nineteenth century Japan does not look like a Third World country. Its long educational traditions, the level of literacy in the key regions of the state, the sophistication of its national and local leadership, its rich and impressive culture, its tradition of easy receipt of new ideas stretching back 1500 years or more, and its relatively advanced artisan and agricultural sectors (in a challenging

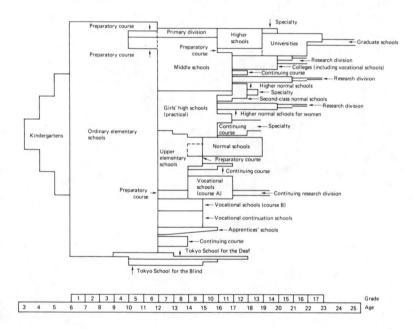

SOURCE From 'Education in Japan', Foreign Press Center, Tokyo 1978.

FIGURE 2.1 *The Japanese Education System in 1919*

physical environment) made it better prepared for industrialisation than any other country outside of Europe or North America. Some initial mistakes were made; for example, Tetsuya Kobayashi (*Society, Schools and Progress in Japan*, Pergamon Press, Oxford 1976, p.27) reminds us that, 'The content of the new education was also in most cases alien to the daily life of the ordinary villagers since it was a direct imitation of elementary schools in the West', but the average Japanese has survived radical change by compromise between the old and the new and the Japanese leadership has usually modified its mistakes, or been taught harshly the error of its ways.

3 'The Excessiveness of Change' (Itō Hirobumi, 1879)

Professor Ken Motoki of Osaka University generously listened to my theory that modern Japanese economic success is built on the excellence of Japanese design, and less on the long working day and the discipline of the work force. This led us to discuss the beauty of the things made in Japan in the past and the continuing tradition of the present. He disappeared to another part of his Department to return with two delicate modern cups, obviously of value, which he presented to me. They were of eye-catching decoration. I was terrified that they would be broken on the trip back to Britain. They made the trip successfully.

Inspired by the gift I went to an antique shop in Kyoto to purchase some early nineteenth-century cups. To persuade me to buy six in a set of eight the dealer cut the price from 4000 yen each to 3500. The following week I returned for the remaining two. '4000 each', the same assistant told me. 'But you charged me 3500 last week'. He smiled at his companion to show that I was pulling a fast one. 'Oh no I didn't', he replied with a smirk. I was about to argue when I realised that I would get nowhere so I paid the 8000 yen asked for. The issue was not what had happened the previous week, but the presence of a colleague.

As in all human affairs the past has a powerful grip on the present, and relationships are always of infinite complexity. It is a singular miracle that ancient countries like Japan and Britain are in continuous change. The secret is to take elements of the past into those changes. Human beings need a sense of continuity. The faster the changes the more we use our extra resources to surround ourselves with the past. How absurd that modern industrial democracies like Japan and Britain have Emperors and Queens, posts from the distant millennia, as heads of state. But what a brilliant way to convince the population that, in the most rapid era of change, nothing is changing. My Imari cups of the early nineteenth century are of breathtaking design, and a reassurance that the past is with me.

The man who sold me the cups showed me in two brief meetings that he was no robot, but yet another idiosyncratic human being trying to cope with close working relationships with equally turbulent people. The Japanese are no different from the British in terms of their eccentricities, strengths, and weaknesses. Myths abound, but people remain their contrary selves. This chapter will explore how Japan began to develop a modern economy despite the weight of history and the all too familiar debates and disagreements which surrounded change. However we care to represent the Japanese they are all too notably members of the human race. We can label them the monsters of the Second World War or the economic supermen of the later twentieth century, but like the rest of us they have their great moments and their low points. One of their more glorious periods was the 60 years following the Meiji Restoration.

Feudalism was abolished in 1871 and national conscription introduced in 1873. Education was looked to as the means to create a modern state around such legislation. But what sort of education? The battle lines were already being drawn up in the latter days of the Tokugawa regime, as has been mentioned. These were the Confucianists, the Western supporters, and the Japan-inspired Kokugakusha. Compromises were sought by many of the advocates who could see no way forward, for example, those supporting a 'Japanese' education suggested that these traditions should be given the central role with Chinese and Western education having an honourable supporting position. Those who came to power after 1868 and the following brief civil war had little doubt that Western learning would have to have a more central role. Even the military, who might be expected to be amongst the most conservative elements in Japanese life, saw a universal education system as necessary to provide good recruits for the army.

Unfortunately for the Western supporters the Meiji Restoration had been brought forward under the motto, 'Revere the Emperor, Throw Out the Barbarian'. Inevitably, this led to expectations that traditional education would not be totally displaced by European learning. The slogan 'Japanese-Chinese-Western Education' might modify the political opposition, but it made for a confusing school system. In 1869 the emerging Tokyo University became the focus of an attempt by the Japanese Education supporters to crush the Confucianists. The following year the same venue saw an alliance of Confucianists and Japanists against the supporters of European knowledge.

The Westerners tended to have the more telling arguments and were politically astute. They gained a majority of places on the School Commission when it was established in late 1868. The 1872 Fundamental Code of Education reaffirmed the priorities of the Westerners with its emphasis on practical objectives.

Both the dying Tokugawa regime and the young enthusiasts of the incoming Meiji Era saw France as the most attractive educational system to copy. The Japanese wanted a centrally controlled model. However, the charge for education was to be more local. Early attempts to get the consumers to pay were of limited success, but then the Ministry of Education turned to prefectures and municipalities. Throughout the last 20 years of the nineteenth century and the first decade of the twentieth the latter covered some 90 per cent of the costs of public education.

With the appointment of Tanaka Fujimaro as Vice-Minister of Education in 1873 and his decision to invite David Murray to act as his adviser, American influence on the curriculum and on teaching methods became apparent, notably in teacher training colleges, the copying of Massachusetts common school ideas, and many areas of vocational education. Textbooks were translated from European and American readers. By the 1870s there were, perhaps, 5000 foreign experts employed in Japan's educational system.

The ambitious plans of the 1872 Code were not to be achieved with the speed hoped for. Japan entered the early years of the twentieth century with two state universities, 222 middle schools, and 27 076 elementary schools. In 1872 four years of compulsory education had been asked for; in the Educational Ordinance of 1879, 16 months; the Revised Educational Ordinance of 1880, three years; the Elementary School Ordinance of 1900, four years; and that of 1907, six years. Japan was a relatively poor country, and neither the national nor the local budgets could raise enough money for the proposed educational programme. Elementary schools had to use old buildings in most cases as there was little cash for new, purpose-built construction. Tokyo University proved immensely expensive. By 1880 only 10 per cent of the teachers had been through a teacher training college. Low salaries often made teaching an unattractive career, although initially samurai found some appeal in it, and particularly if they could not get government, army or police jobs.

An educational system dominated by untrained and old style teachers often unable to cope with the new, Western curriculum found in rural areas that school attendance was erratic. Poor families stated that the compulsory school fees were difficult to raise (in 1900 education was made free), books too expensive, and often accused the education of being irrelevant to their children's way of life. Farmers needed their children's labour at certain times of the year, and the poor of Tokyo or Osaka or Kyoto wanted their sons in employment by the time they were ten or 11. The 1870s were notable for popular conservative rebellions against conscription, the solar calendar, and schools. Often the latter were seen as establishments for supplying the army.

The Meiji opinion leaders had aimed at producing a modern state whilst trying to control rapid social change. The crushing of the conservative armed rebellions of the 1870s then faced the government with a demand for parliamentary democracy. Western-style personal liberty came into vogue with certain pressure groups. At the same time the increasingly conservative Nishimura Shigeki made his educational survey (1877) which recommended a shorter school year, either more modest or no tuition charges, and a curriculum closer to people's daily lives (for example, girls taught domestic skills such as sewing).

The Education Ordinance of 1879 illustrated the Minister of Education Tanaka's belief that the educational objectives of central government could be implemented under local control in a manner to meet local conditions. Some concessions to teacher autonomy were encouraged, corporal punishment in schools forbidden, teacher rotation to aid poorly staffed schools provided for, and, as previously noted, compulsory education was shortened to 16 months between the ages of six and 14 years. There is much evidence to suggest that Tanaka was influenced in these proposals by his American adviser David Murray. The opposition to such Western ideas as local autonomy and the cult of the individual was to be substantial.

The most distinguished opponent of Tanaka's Western-inspired liberalism was the Emperor Meiji. After a tour of a number of areas of Japan in 1878 he was distressed by some of the educational developments he saw. Motoda Eifu, his Confucian Lecturer, was instructed to compose a statement on 'The Great Principles of Education' (Kyōgaku Taishi). This was published as an Imperial Rescript in 1879 and immediately became a flagship of the conservative opposition.

Initially the Council of Elders who advised the Emperor received the new Education Ordinance without serious opposition, but in the following month Itō Hirobumi was instructed to redraft the

Ordinance to take into account the Kyōgaku Taishi, and its claim that the Westernisation of education had gone too far. Itō reacted with hostility, seeing Motoda's initiative as likely to lead to further political meddling under the claim of Imperial interest. Itō issued his 'Opinion on Education' (Kyōiku-gi). He challenged Motoda's belief that the schools were to blame for the country's supposed moral disorder, 'In sum, then, the damage to our customs comes from *the excessiveness of the change*, and it was inevitable. In our anxiety over the general situation, therefore, we should not blame the new educational system for everything. Educational legislation is only one of the remedies for the situation. Since education is not the principal cause of the failure, it can be no more than an indirect cure. Education is a long-term cure; immediate results should not be demanded of it'. Itō was not a liberal, but he wished the Emperor to be above the day-to-day wranglings of government. The Ordinance was promulgated on 29 September. Itō also abolished the post of Confucian Lecturer to the Emperor. The conservative reaction was swift and with some effect. In 1880 Tanaka had to resign, and a new Educational Ordinance based on Motoda's views replaced that of the previous year.

The new Ordinance put morals at the centre of the school curriculum. The 1881 Memorandum for Elementary School Teachers had as its first article, 'In order to guide people, make them good, give them wide knowledge, and to do this wisely, teachers must particularly stress moral education to their pupils. Loyalty to the Imperial House, love of country, filial piety towards parents, respect for superiors, faith in friends, charity towards inferiors, and respect for oneself constitute the great path of human morality. The teacher must himself be a model of these virtues in his daily life, and must endeavour to stimulate his pupils along the path of virtue'. Of course, it is important to remember that many European and North American school systems of the nineteenth century were built on similar sentiments. During his 12 years of guiding the Massachusetts educational revival of the 1830s and 1840s Horace Mann, for example, wrote in his annual reports of the need for teachers to be moral paragons and for the schools to fashion good citizens.

From 1880 the translation of foreign books on morality for schools was prohibited. The same year provincial officers were appointed to inspect textbooks. A number of books were banned as likely to promote social disorder. New books were prepared to teach morality. The conservative regime curbed the independence of teachers and proclaimed them public servants. Teachers after 1880 could not attend political meetings.

The liberal faction had changed the battlefield from education. In late 1881 the government was forced to publish an Imperial Rescript saying that they would set up a national assembly in 1890. As with all agriculturally-based economies of the nineteenth century Japan was particularly vulnerable to changing economic conditions, and the early 1880s was notable for a depression which heightened social tension. The ideological battles of the Westerners, Japanists, and Confucianists were given further edge.

Itō, whilst no supporter of the Confucianists, or even the Japanists, found much to worry him in the Western influences. He was on the side of the state, not the individual, and wanted Western materialism made subservient to traditional Japanese public morality. His European tour tended to confirm his prejudices, as foreign travel often does. When he was in Paris in September of 1882, the Japanese Minister in London, Mori Arinori, visited him. They found they shared similar views on the role of education in the making of the new Japan. Itō promised Mori that he would make him Minister of Education. In July of 1884 Mori returned to Japan. In December 1885 Japan introduced government by Cabinet with Itō as the first Prime Minister. In the face of virulent conservative opposition Mori was appointed Education Minister.

In 1886 Mori established the foundations of his educational system. The School Decree on Elementary Education re-established compulsory education as four years, although three years could be claimed under special circumstances. The Imperial University Decree defined the role of Tokyo University and added 'Imperial' to its title. A Middle School Decree saw an upper and lower division established; the former later became the university preparatory higher school.

Despite having flirted with Westernism Mori was a nationalist who stated publicly many times that the education system was for the benefit of the state, not of the students. Ironically, Mori was to be assassinated in 1889 by a youthful nationalist.

Mori, as a nationalist, had to combine the Western style of sceptical thinking which produced unique achievements in science and technology, with the Meiji leadership's desire to rule by political absolutism. To be a great power Japan would have to build a modern, science-based economy, but Imperial government wanted a docile population. The education system had to reconcile what in Britain would have been seen as irreconcilable. Mori's solution lasted until

1945. The compulsory education system was drenched in an atmosphere of nationalism and moral exhortation. On top of this there was created an élite university sector given remarkable academic freedom. Mori gambled on the indoctrination of the school system curbing the dangers for the relatively small numbers going forward to the intellectual exhilaration of university study.

Mori side-stepped the moral teachings of the Confucianists for a morality related to his view of national needs. The schools were to teach the new citizenry their prime commitment to the well-being of the state. The Emperor would be used as a tool to reinforce this. A milder form of this could be found in British schools during the height of the Empire at the end of the nineteenth century and during the first decades of the twentieth century.

Mori's nationalist views were best epitomised by his regime for teacher training colleges (Normal Schools). The students were given state grants and placed under military discipline. Like a British public school they aimed at character-training as much as intellectual development. Each teacher training college had to arrange six hours of military drill each week and many of the principals were regular army officers. Much was made of the virtue of obedience. Surprisingly, many of Mori's ideas were taken from the Swedenborgian Thomas Lake Harris with whom Mori had spent time in America in 1867. Harris's utopians of The Brotherhood of the New Life had as their motto 'Dignity, Friendship, and Obedience' which Mori high-jacked as the slogan for the Normal Schools in Japan.

My father had seven sisters and I recall from the moment of my first awareness that I trusted implicitly their truthfulness. The Stephens' family would not tell lies. In my adulthood I have not had such cause for confidence in other people. My aunts' word could be accepted without even a moment's thought. They were the products of Cornish non-conformity, parents imbued with high moral values, and local schools which reinforced those priorities. After 1945 life seemed much more complicated and morality fragmented into a million doubts and counter-arguments.

Mori's efforts at establishing a certain style of education appear to have taken further the ambitions of the Victorians to have a truthful, and law abiding citizenry. He accepted the moral objectives of utopian Christians as well suited to the traditions of Japan's past and the style of political future he felt it needed. Whilst the Confucianists accused him of being a Christian it was not the religious belief he sought to transfer to Japan, but the high moral standards and self-discipline.

The Normal Schools were attractive to students who could not get into the university. They were primarily aimed at producing schoolteachers, but became also noted as a route to other key posts in Japanese society such as the Army, and local government. A modernising economy had an increasing appetite for the highly educated, and initially the universities did not produce enough graduates.

Most of the participants in higher education in the nineteenth century came from the samuri class. Traditionally the samuri had a low opinion of commerce and an equal distaste for getting their hands dirty. The merchant and labouring classes before 1868 had been viewed with contempt. Again, in Britain it has taken engineering a long time to acquire esteem. A study of law or the humanities has been more fashionable than mechanical engineering. In Meiji Japan to graduate in law from Tokyo University led to such highly prized opportunities as central government service. Japan was faced by its brightest and best wanting to follow the pre-Meiji Restoration ideal of a cultivated gentleman. Post-Industrial Revolution Britain had a lot in common with industrialising Japan.

The Japanese position over doing anything which involved dirtying the hands was more extreme than the British avoidance of careers thought of as rule-of-thumb men's work. The Japanese wanted to get a civil service job. The high-flyers endeavoured to study Law at Tokyo University in order to achieve this. It was 1915 before the rest of the University equalled in size the Law Faculty.

As in Victorian Britain, many of the Japanese leaders proclaimed the importance of science and technology. Whilst the Westerners saw practical education as the acquiring of such things as technical skills to promote a modern economy, the Confucianists proclaimed its importance as it fitted into their traditional belief that people should be educated to fit their station in life. Women should be prepared for the role of housewife. Those in the rural areas should have an education which fitted them to labour in the fields. The lower orders should be given only the amount and style of education to get by as a useful citizen. In Tokugawa Japan the in-service apprenticeship had been used to train the young. The new schooling would take away some of the time previously so used. A conservative society was reluctant to bring technical education into the education sector.

To begin its modernisation Meiji Japan relied on the limited numbers of people who had Western knowledge, but they were so few that it was quickly decided to send young men abroad to be trained in the necessary skills. Of the first educational budget well over 10 per cent was spent on such overseas study. Many Japanese also studied abroad using private funding. As it was so expensive as soon as there were enough overseas educated experts then Japan established its own institutions. A further substantial expense was incurred by bringing in foreign experts to act as teachers and advisers. At the beginning of the new government the Ministry of Industry was using 50 per cent of its budget on salaries for foreigners. To train its personnel the Ministry of Public Works in 1871 founded a school and technical college totally staffed by Britons and saw 58 per cent of its budget taken up by this initiative.

As with other modern educational developments technical and vocational education in Japan could build on some Tokugawa precedents. The merchants had taught their children commercial subjects, and the apprenticeship system was often of some sophistication. This helped to disguise the slow provision of Western technical and commercial education. The shortage of trained personnel only became glaring during and after the Sino-Japanese War. Some of the private companies from the 1870s onwards set-up their own training schemes.

The Sino-Japanese War of 1894–95 saw the Education Minister Inoue Kowashi much perplexed by the poor quality of technician education. He recognised world competition as mainly economic, not military, and considered that Japan had plenty of good generals in industry, but not enough corporals and sergeants. He put a Vocational Education Law through the Diet in 1894. Over the next decade or so vocational schools at the lower secondary level were established, to be followed by upper secondary and junior college level technical institutions. This formalised into the Special School (semmongakko) and the Higher Technical School (koto-semmongakko). Their graduates included engineers, dentists, draughtsmen and accountants, but they lacked the prestige of the universities. As in Britain, technical education was the poor cousin of higher education.

Also as in Britain the emerging factory system had an insatiable appetite for female labour. Alongside a demand for greater numbers of women in factories than men went a rapid expansion of clerical jobs. Girls were thereby encouraged to attend elementary education in similar numbers to boys. Again like Britain, secondary school provision for girls was very slow in coming. However, in 1899 the Higher Girls' School Law was passed, aimed at providing at least one middle school for females in each prefecture. By 1900 women could take examinations to become medics and the first medical school for women was opened. In 1901 the Japan's Women's University was founded, although it was misnamed as it was at a lower academic level. The Tohoku Imperial University when established in 1906 was permitted to admit some women students. Such initiatives are somewhat misleading as it was not until after the Second World War that women achieved the beginnings of equality of opportunity in higher education.

Amongst my most enjoyable lecturing experiences was that at Ochanomizu University, at the invitation of my friend Takeshi Ogawa. It is one of two national universities for women in Japan and its history illustrates the development of female higher education. Its roots are in the Tokyo Normative School established in 1874 to train women teachers. This was Japan's first higher education institution for women. In 1886 it was made the Department for Women of the Tokyo Higher Normal School. It became independent again in 1890 as the Tokyo Women's Higher Normal School. The School was located at Ochanomizu. As with so many higher education institutions over the last hundred years it took on new roles and research obligations, but suffered a set-back in 1923 when the severe earthquake of that year destroyed its original site and it had to move to Otsuka where its new buildings were opened in 1930. After 1945 it began again as Ochanomizu University, and today has the three Faculties of Letters and Education, Science, and Home Economics.

The Japanese entered the twentieth century with a centralised educational bureaucracy loosely based on the French model, elementary schools which were co-educational and inspired by American practice, and a university sector which owed much to Germany. The teacher training colleges also looked to an American model.

The emerging system, which was to last until 1945, was of six years of elementary education, after which the pupils were streamed into various alternatives from which it was difficult to switch. Middle schools were not co-educational. For females there were Girls' High Schools. Boys might finish their education at the elementary school, whilst in contrast about 10 per cent would eventually try for higher education. The move from middle school to higher school was difficult as there were places for only about 7 per cent of middle school graduates. Perhaps half of the higher schools were seen as a route into the Imperial universities. These encouraged a ruthless competition for places. In the 1920s there were about 5000 places each year at the 33 key higher schools to which the universities looked for students. There were 70 000 middle school graduates. Second-chance education was limited with some using the licensing examination (kenteishiken) to get into a higher school, or the normal school programme to go to a higher normal school and then, after 1929, onto the two universities of arts and sciences.

The higher school lasted for three years prior to university. For others they might finish their education, or go to a military or normal school, or a college or higher technical school. Despite a view in prewar Japan that foreign higher education was inferior, many young people who could not get into a Japanese university went abroad to study. On return such graduates found themselves at a disadvantage to those who had attended Japanese universities when it came to employment in the civil service or business. As with the young man at Tokyo University who informed me that Japanese academics had to have Japanese higher degrees so the society of the early twentieth century favoured Japanese graduates over the Japanese who had studied abroad. This was not just chauvinism, although, as today, doubtlessly there was an element of nationalism in such discrimination, but a recognition that a ruthlessly competitive educational system saw 'the best' going to the Imperial universities. Why choose a Harvard Law School graduate who had not been able to get into the Law Faculty of Tokyo Imperial University when you could appoint someone who had?

As today, in the Japan of, say, the 1920s those leaving the elementary schools knew which were the best middle schools to get them into the most distinguished higher schools. Just as attendance at prewar Eton was more likely to get a pupil into Oxford so the classic route into Tokyo Imperial University was via First Middle School in Tokyo and then First Higher School in Tokyo. Unlike England, the great schools were government-funded ones. The national order of distinction was First Higher School in Tokyo, followed by Third Higher School in Tokyo and then Second Higher School in Tokyo.

The Imperial universities were the cream of the 45 prewar universities. At the pinnacle was Tokyo with its main challenge coming from Kyoto. After the golden duo came the other government universities and some distinguished private institutions. At the bottom of the pyramid were some 23 private universities. Tokyo Imperial

University took the cream of the students from the most eminent of the government higher schools. However, those who graduated from the government higher schools could be fairly sure of a place at one of the prestigious universities.

Of course, it is also important to stress that within a University like Tokyo certain subjects and faculties were harder to get into than others. Tokyo established Faculties of Law, Science, Letters and Medicine in 1877, Agriculture and Engineering in 1914, and Economics in 1919. Its great rival Kyoto Imperial University began with Faculties of Science and Engineering in 1897, and then Faculties of Law and Medicine in 1899, and Letters in 1906. As we have seen the greatest prestige in Japan's most fashionable University went to the Faculty of Law. That was the ultimate objective of any ambitious young male in the pre-1930 Japanese educational system.

As with a number of European educational systems, Japan had a fiercely competitive schools' tradition which produced an indisputably male élite. Again like its European counterparts, once the student had made it to the university it was difficult not to get the graduate qualification which would guarantee entry into one of the most favoured of careers. The university student could take life easily, although that is not to say that many did not work hard.

Such a ruthlessly competitive educational system meant that in many of the years prior to the Second World War of every thousand pupils entering elementary school perhaps only three would eventually graduate from university. Of course, there were other reasons in Japan for dropping out before university. As in prewar Europe and North America, perhaps a majority of parents could not support their children for such a long period of study. It was not just a question of whether they gained scholarships to cover the cost of the education, but of families denied another wage coming into a household.

The changing nature of Japanese society after 1868 is usefully illustrated by the universities. In his book *Society, Schools and Progress in Japan* (Pergamon Press, Oxford 1976, pp.112–13) Professor Tetsuya Kobayashi of Kyoto University summarises:

> How the graduates formed themselves into an élite group of Japanese society was shown chronologically in a study conducted by Professor Aso Yutaka based on several editions of a Japanese 'Who's Who'. According to Professor Azabu's study, university graduates formed only 20% of the élite group in 1903. The percentage remained about the same until the latter part of the 1920s;

25% in 1911 and 1915 respectively, and 21% in 1921. In the late 1920s the figure increased rapidly; 39% in 1928, 40% in 1934, and 50% in 1941. After the end of World War II university graduates became the majority of the élite group, 81% in 1957, and 83% in 1964. Over the half century which the study covered, the nature of the élite group in the Japanese study has thus changed; the traditional types in the élite, such as aristocrats and landowners, decreased in numbers and finally disappeared, while the intellectual élite, such as professors, educators, and artists, increased. The business leaders and bureaucrats constantly occupied an important and substantial part of the élite group.

Although it has been suggested that Japan was more akin to a Second World country in the nineteenth century it rightly saw itself as a latecomer to the push for First World economic characteristics. No country in attempting such development has placed more emphasis on education as a central vehicle for success. If education was to be so important then those who underwent it might expect to do well from such early investment of their time, effort and, mainly, family financial resources. What was the point of getting your Tokyo Imperial University law degree if you found the key vacancies in the civil service filled by the sons of aristocrats?

Okuma Shigenobu, creator of Waseda University in 1900, proclaimed at the thirteen anniversary of the founding of that institution, 'In general there are not many students who can go to college. They constitute a minority. It is this small minority of students who set the example for the nation at large. They are the leaders of the nation. They are the strength of the nation. They form the foundation for the steady progress of the nation. They are the ones who become the vanguards of civilizing enterprises. In order to become a model citizen, knowledge alone is not sufficient; the building of a moral personality is necessary'. Would the education system deliver men of good character to lead all areas of Japanese life during the turmoil of the 1930s and 1940s? The 15 years from 1930 to 1945 might have disheartened a less robust people.

4 'We Stand for Divine Rulership.' Japan and Education in the 1930-45 Period

As in many other countries, the impact of the West on Japan in the nineteenth century led to a nationalistic reaction. Proud, and particularly relatively self-contained, cultures of distinguished history easily resented the unique shock of European technology. Japan might have borrowed heavily from China and Korea in the distant past, but the initiative was usually taken from its side. Europe and its satellite North America came crashing in upon Japan in a way it had never before experienced. Japan from the sixteenth century had been aware of Europe; after all Portuguese trade and missionary activity had started there in the 1540s, but it was the British creation of the Industrial Revolution which made the West's intrusion in the nineteenth century of unparalleled severity. The gap between the level of Japan's economy and that of Britain was dramatic. The Industrial Revolution had brought in a quite new meaning to the term 'contemporary technology'; surprise at such achievements as steam power in Japan was always in danger of bringing in its wake an inferiority complex which for a sizeable minority fuelled ultranationalism.

Amongst a ferment of such nationalistic reaction in 1901 the Amur Society had been founded. Japan, used to borrowing other people's technology, had begun to gather momentum as an industrialising power from the 1880s, but its acceptance of Western political ideas was more superficial. Not until after 1945 did Japan's hierarchical society take to democracy. As we have seen, prior to 1945 the debate might be vigorous, and membership of the hierarchies changing, but it was still a very traditional nation. Unlike Britain the Government took a central role in industrialisation, and decisions were always influenced by military requirements. Japan intended to remain independent, and its army and navy would ensure this by its use of European technology. Military men were notable members of the Amur Society and greatly favoured its objective of throwing

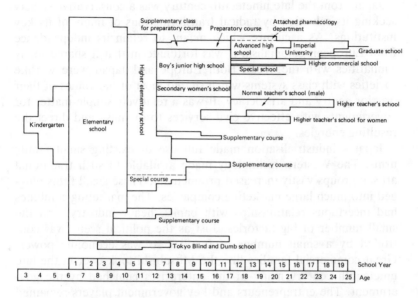

Supplementary class for preparatory course
Preparatory course
Attached pharmacology department
Advanced high school
Imperial University
Graduate school
Higher commercial school
Boy's junior high school
Special school
Secondary women's school
Normal teacher's school (male)
Higher teacher's school
Higher teacher's school for women
Kindergarten
Elementary school
Higher elementary school
Supplementary course
Supplementary course
Special course
Supplementary course
Tokyo Blind and Dumb school

| 1 | 2 | 3 | 4 | 5 | 6 | 7 | 8 | 9 | 10 | 11 | 12 | 13 | 14 | 15 | 16 | 17 | 18 | 19 | School Year |

| 3 | 4 | 5 | 6 | 7 | 8 | 9 | 10 | 11 | 12 | 13 | 14 | 15 | 16 | 17 | 18 | 19 | 20 | 21 | 22 | 23 | 24 | 25 | Age |

FIGURE 4.1 *The School System in 1892*

the Europeans out of Asia. Such ambitions under Japanese direction were heady wine for the nationalists. It becomes easier to understand how the military drifted into expansionist plans in Asia. To free Asia might mean first controlling it territorially.

The opening words of the Amur Society's 1930 anniversary statement are, 'We Stand for Divine Rulership. Basing ourselves on the fundamental teachings of the foundation of the Empire, we seek the extension of the Imperial influence to all peoples and places and the fulfilment of the glory of our national policy'. Although Japan had introduced universal male suffrage in 1925 which had thrown up new political leaders to rival the established clans and inner groups, the military in the 1930s provided cliques of considerable influence. Despite such democratic legislation and the expansion of the military (Japan had acquired Korea in 1910 and Manchuria in 1931–32) much political power remained in traditional hands. The Emperor was a key symbol of such continuity. Like many societies before it, Japan responded to such a uniting and powerful figurehead whilst many of its citizens were seduced by the imperial dream.

Japan from the late nineteenth century was a conservative society seeking its salvation by radical transformations of many of its key institutions. As a culture which meant to retain its independence from European colonialism it was fortunate in that it shared many similarities with the West. Both Europe and Japan were warlike societies with class systems which shared most of the values of their warrior gentry and aristocracy. It was a relatively simple matter for governments with effective civil services to organise and direct the resulting energies.

Japan's industrialisation made full use of existing small family firms. The Western technology made available to such traditional artisan groups vastly increased productivity. These small firms plugged into much large marketing companies. The marketing combines had incestuous relationships with banks, heavy industry, and the small number of big factories. Just as the political scene was controlled by a small number of families so was economic power. Great commercial families like the Mitsubishi took over in the late nineteenth century many of the enterprises launched by the government. The entrepreneurs and key government players remained closely allied, and marriage between the two groups was frequent. Whilst the government was willing to give to, for example, Mitsui for a peppercorn price expensively established plant, in return politicians expected industrialists to be willing to set up factories considered necessary to the state. The original house rules of the Mitsubishi Company (Article 4) stated, 'Operate all enterprises with the national interest in mind'. It helped that the founding families of Japan's economic oligarchy were sometimes of samurai origin.

The samurai traditions behind the leadership which pulled Japan rapidly from a largely feudal society to an industrial country favoured the West's war-making abilities based on the manufacturing techniques pioneered and perfected by Britain's Industrial Revolution. The changes of incomparable profundity were instituted within a single generation. The West's industrialisation was a remarkably leisurely affair in comparison. Social discipline was sustained by the use of traditional values and, above all else, the symbol of the Emperor. A surrounding mythology was polished and extended. The traditional élites in the nineteenth century must have blessed the day the Tokugawa freebooters in the early seventeenth century had accepted the need for the separate continuing existence of the Imperial household. The Japanese duality of the ruling shoguns and the powerless emperors permitted change of unique dimension with the ending of Tokugawa government, and the majority acceptance of 'Westernisation', under the symbolic guise of power being given back to the Emperor. The Emperor was permitted less real power than he appeared to have. The Divine Rulership was the justification of the extension of the power of the traditional élites, and those who were able to join them as the Japanese economy and its Asian extensions developed.

The Amur Society proclaimed, 'Developing the plan of the founders of Japan, we will widen the Great Way of Eastern culture, work out a harmony of Eastern and Western cultures, and take the lead amongst the peoples of Asia'. The intention was to ' . . . . end many evils, such as the formal exaltation of the law which restricts the people's freedom, and inhibits commonsense solutions, encourages inefficiency in public and private life, and undermines proper constitutional government. A return to full imperial government will be sought'. The ultranationalist quality of the society was well demonstrated by the objectives, 'We shall rebuild the present administrative system. We will develop overseas expansion through our diplomacy, further the people's prosperity by internal reforms, and solve labour and management problems by the establishment of new social policies. Thereby we will strengthen the Empire's foundations. We shall carry out the spirit of the Imperial Rescript of Soldiers and Sailors and stimulate a martial spirit by working towards the goal of a nation in arms. Thereby we look towards the perfection of national defence'.

For such nationalists, education was the obvious vehicle, 'We plan a fundamental reform of the present educational system, which is copied from those of Europe and America; we shall set up a basic study of a national education with origins in our national polity. Thereby we anticipate the further development and improvement of the wisdom and virtue of the Yamato race'.

The great Cornish engineer Richard Trevithick (1771–1833) had invented the railway engine in 1801 when he demonstrated the first steam locomotive to run on rails. By 1874 there were 104 foreign railway engineers in Japan (94 of them British) including the famed inventor's grandson, Richard Francis Trevithick (1845–1913). The grandson organised the first manufacture of railway engines in Japan. The first railway line had been constructed, funded by a loan of a million pounds raised in London (at 9 per cent interest per annum), from Tokyo to Yokohama using British engineers and surveyors. The Emperor opened the railway which used British trains and equipment, on 14 October 1872. Initially all key staff, from engine drivers to ticket collectors, were British. The Japanese were able students and by 1888 Japanese railways employed only 14 foreigners.

The example of the introduction of railway technology to Japan usefully illustrates a number of points already referred to. Very shortly after the Meiji Restoration, Japan was introducing the most sophisticated of engineering from the West. The contrast between what was being attempted and traditional Japan could not have been made more simply. The British overseeing the construction of the first railway lines complained about the insistence of the numerous samurai in the labour force on wearing their habitual two swords (the wearing of swords was forbidden after 1876), the steel of which affected the magnetic surveying compasses. Whilst the Japanese were quick to learn the various techniques of the Industrial Revolution, their pre-industrial outlook either remained or was modified less than in the West. The groups like the Amur Society were the result. Traditional Japan was protecting itself against Western Imperialism by the remarkably rapid absorbing of European and North American technology. Education reflected this ambivalence towards the West. The debate was over how to import European or American educational techniques to make it more effective, whilst retaining a 'Japanese' content. The attempt to retain their 'Japaneseness' led the 'Yamato race' to be expansionist and to absorb those things from the West which would increase their material power. The railways symbolised the age of steam, the epitome of mechanical power replacing muscle power, and were bound to be an early importation.

The army in Japan became a focus of attention between change and stasis. A decision had been taken to create a European-style force. The resulting conscription from all the traditional classes of Japan, peasants, merchants and samurai, saw unusual opportunities opening for a minority. Officers were treated with a deference previously accorded to local gentry. Unlike the aristocratic officer corps of the Imperial Navy, army officers were frequently recruited from other than the samurai class. A peasant of ability could become an officer and thereby inherit the former samurai's standing. Such men were outside established social hierarchies, and junior army officers made a notable element in ultranationalist groups. In this they doubtless reflected the rural opinion from which they sprang.

Such junior army officers were not restrained by an allegiance to the traditional hierarchies, and provided the most effective of the nation's extremists. The 1930s saw them manipulating the threat of popular revolution to their own ends and challenging party politicians. Deeds of violence became commonplace. They could be seen as the beginnings of a malign 'democratic' revolution which was to push Japan into war with China, and eventually the West. Even within the junior officer ranks of the Army there were many variations of ultranationalist outlook. These ranged from Imperialists to Asia Liberationists. What gave them cohesion was the belief that Japan was unique, its Emperor divine, and that their country had a national mission of greatness. Prewar education was expected to shape these objectives, and the focus got sharper the further into the 1930s Japan progressed.

When the Ministry of Education in 1937 printed and distributed millions of copies of 'The Principles of the National Polity' the influence of the ultranationalists on education became crystal clear: ' . . . the Emperors hand over the august injunctions of the Imperial Ancestors, and thereby make clear the great principle of the founding of the nation and the great Way which the people should follow. Here lies the basic principle of our education. Wherefore, education, too, is in its essence united with the religious rites and government. In short, religious rites, government and education, each fulfilling its function, are entirely one'. Of education, the document states later that it 'comprises the spirit of guarding and maintaining the prosperity of the Imperial Throne by following the august spirit manifested in the founding of the Empire in keeping with our national entity. Hence, this is entirely different in its essence from the mere development and perfection of oneself such as is seen in the idea of self-realisation and perfection of one's character as set forth in individualistic pedagogics. In short, it is not a mere development of individual minds and faculties set apart from the nation, but the rearing of a people manifesting the Way of our nation. Education, whose object is the cultivation of the creative faculties of individuals or the development of individual characteristics, is liable to be biased toward individuals and to be led by individual inclinations, and in the long run to fall into an unplanned education, and to run counter to the principles of the education of our country . . . . . it is to be noted that the true object of our national education is seen in walking the Way of the founding of our Empire with knowledge and practice united in one'.

The reaction against the import of Western ideas in education which had first substantially been observed in the 1860s notably had support amongst the scholars of the Chinese classics. Confucianism underpinned many of the so-called traditionalists' arguments. This was further fuelled by the new nationalism of the 1880s. As has been noted, there was an insistence on the moral training being paramount. The government was expected to decide how morality would be taught, and then to ensure it was adequately administered within the schools. As such moral training under government control had been frowned upon in much of Europe and in North America, those who looked to the West and modernisation rightly regarded this as a key issue if Japan was to change.

A major battle between the feudalistic Confucian ideology and modern Western rationalism was bound to be fought over the introduction of European science and technology. The initial advocates of scientific education were samurai, and, correctly, their views were seen as the most dangerous of attacks on the established class system.

The reformers looked to basic theoretical physics as the vehicle to convert Japan to modern science. The traditionalists promoted the Confucian view of nature as an alternative. Scientific education saw natural history gaining at the expense of physics. Confucian morality and practical knowledge were favoured in order to produce for the Emperor obedient elementary school pupils. Scientific understanding was pushed to one side under the 1886 elementary school reforms which combined all the science subjects, previously taught separately, into a single one called 'rika'. It was allocated fewer teaching hours (usually two hours per week during the final four years of the eight years of elementary education). The 1891 General Rules of Teaching Elementary Education shaped rika for the period up to the end of the Second World War. The General Rules stated: 'The major purpose of rika is the cultivation of minds that love nature through a precise observation of nature and natural phenomena and the acquisition of general knowledge of their interrelations and relationship with the life of people. In the early stages of education, emphasis should be placed on teaching the facts regarding plants, animals, minerals, and natural phenomena in the school's locality that can be empirically observed by the schoolchildren and then progress to the acquisition of general knowledge of the shape, structure, life, and growth of important plants and animals through observation. Also, depending on the school grade, let children understand the interrelations between plants and animals and their relationship with the life of people, ordinary physical and chemical phenomena, and the structure and motion of ordinary machines they may encounter. Furthermore, let them acquire a general knowledge of human physiology and health. Rika should emphasise as much as possible the teaching of items useful for the people's life when engaged in farming, industry, and other fields; teaching about plants and animals in particular should aim at instilling general knowledge about important production methods that may be related to them. Rika also requires live observation, or demonstration of specimens, models, and drawings, or simple examinations to provide children with a clearer understanding'.

The First World War made less tenable the rika approach. Science and technology moved centre stage for the players in the beginning of modern post-Industrial Revolution conflict. The astute noted the advantages gained by those with a good science education based on a rational approach. Towards the end of the war the Japanese government was making available extra finance for the teaching of chemistry and physics in secondary schools and teacher training colleges. In 1917 the Ministry of Education stated, 'Today, it is urgent that we encourage research in physics and chemistry and spread this knowledge among the people, to enhance industrial production and the sound development of those industries contributing to the strengthening of national power. It is vital to the future of the nation that school education in physics and chemistry be implemented according to this principle, and that teaching methods be improved further, with particular emphasis placed on experiments. Excessive adherence to method and indoctrination should be avoided as much as possible; efforts should be focussed rather on the precise acquisition of knowledge appropriate to the actual life of the people and the cultivation of a creative and spontaneous spirit'.

To aid the teaching of science in elementary schools in particular in 1918 the Scientific Education Research Council was established. The following year science teaching was commenced in the fourth grade (previously elementary schools had not started it until the fifth grade), and the number of hours devoted to chemistry and physics in the secondary schools were increased.

The British way of teaching science by students carrying out experiments after the First World War found favour in the Ministry of Education. Previously Japanese educators had looked to Germany for example. Progress was slow, despite official approval, because of poorly prepared teachers. Science teachers continued to favour such German educationalists as Johann Friedrich Herbart with his five stages of preparation, presentation comparison, summarisation, and application.

The Great Depression of the early 1930s saw a slow down of Japan's economic development leading to popular disillusionment with industry, science and technology. An increasingly vocal work force added to the sense of national instability amongst the ruling élites. There was much talk in governmental circles of the need to cultivate a Japanese spirit, and to use education to create a right thinking citizenry. Japan's leadership found itself desiring to promote education in science and technology whilst pursuing the contrary objective of the irrational theme of 'the Japanese spirit'. A lobby inevitably developed amongst scientific educationalists which claimed that the scientifically-trained mind was ideally suited to guide public thought.

There were calls for further increases in the time allocated to science teaching, and a plea that in the elementary schools it should be more closely related to the lives and experiences of the children. A Marxist based working class political movement in the early 1930s under such men as Hidehiko Wakita promoted the cause of modern, Western science for the school system. With the suppression of such lobbies during the 1930s rika remained less altered than it needed to be.

The Sino-Japanese War which commenced in 1937, and notably the Pacific War in 1941, re-established national interest in science education. If the first of the modern wars had been the Great War of 1914–18, then the Second World War gave further emphasis to the overwhelming importance of science and technology. The Japanese government continued to seek some sort of unity between the contradictory objectives of the promotion of 'the Japanese spirit' and the need for an effective teaching of science. Amongst others, Kunihiko Hashida, a physiologist, supported the notion of a 'scientific approach in the Japanese way'. He advocated the slogan 'Science as Conduct'. He combined the Western scientific tradition with both Confucian and Eastern Buddhist thought. Spiritual values were to stand alongside Western rationalism. He served as Minister of Education from 1940 to 1943.

As total war loomed the elementary schools were re-organised into national schools in 1941. Schools were for the 'basic training of the people through ordinary elementary education in conformity with the morality of the Empire'. A diverse school curriculum was streamlined into just four courses – National Morality, Science and

Mathematics, National Arts and Physical Training. Science education began in the first grade. By 1944 the Ministry of Education was encouraging the training of gifted children in special science education in elementary schools attached to Higher Teachers' Schools. Further emphasis on science and military education was given within secondary education.

Whilst the conflict between Western rationalism and pre-Meiji Restoration spiritual values is well illustrated by Japan's need to accept science and technology in its educational curriculum, equally painful in the move to modernise the country was the field of civic ethics. Education had to prepare the Japanese to be citizens in a capitalist industrial society. Issues of personal freedom, greater equality, choice and similar themes had to be introduced whilst attempting to maintain social stability. All countries experiencing industrialisation have found difficult the accommodation of the social changes which come with the move from being a rural to an urban society. Japan suffered greatly from this and other, related changes.

As we have seen, the Confucian morality of Japan's feudal past retained great influence up to 1945. Japan saw itself as having to modernise to avoid becoming a Western colony, but many of its leaders disliked Western ideas of equality, or similar individual rights. Education was expected to produce a standard Japanese citizen who would be obedient to the government. Under such circumstances it is easy to understand how education came to stress loyalty to the Emperor. The Emperor was a symbol of unity, and a guarantee of unchanging values during a time of great change. Initially the 'Five Articles of the Imperial Oath' and similar proclamations of the 1870s illustrated the interest of those in power in exploring such Western-promoted ideas as equality of citizens and public opinion influencing state decisions. Education was to help each citizen 'Attain social independence, manage property, and enrich life'.

In his work 'What is Moral Education?' Fukuzawa had written in 1882, 'The government and the general public are unanimously striving for the advancement of the nation. And the consciousness of the people pursuing and endeavouring to attain individual independence has become a stern and solid one. It is important in today's education, which stresses sovereign independence, to give due priority to the independence of individuals, thereby maintaining relations with others and the social order. In other words, one's independence depends on respect for the independence of others, which in turn makes possible the independence of a nation.

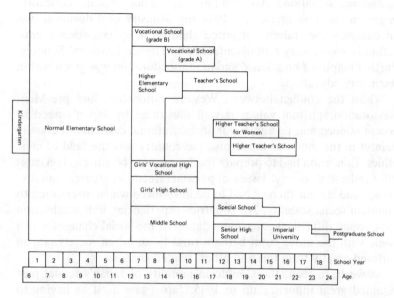

FIGURE 4.2 *The School System in 1910*

This principle of individual independence can apply to every case, whether it is the loyalty to the Emperor, whether it is filial devotion to parents, whether it is deferring to seniority, or whether it is winning the confidence of friends'. From such relatively broad approaches to modernisation an increasingly anxious government chose to stress loyalty to the Emperor and filial duty as the centrepieces of Japanese citizenship. Mori, when first Minister of Education, might suggest that education in ethics should be secular and that 'a general view of human society teaches us that the world is based on mutual reliance between oneself and others, and which, in fact, constitutes the eternal peace of the world', but the traditionalists were unlikely to have much sympathy with such views.

The explorations in ethics of the late nineteenth and early twentieth century were largely culminated as the government faced such unnerving modern movements as an increasingly materialistic general public influenced by nationalism of raw dimensions and with many flirting with various forms of socialism. In 1910 school texts were revised to emphasise further commitment to family and Emperor.

New international trends, however, had an impact on Japan. From 1912 to 1926 the Taisho Era reflected the industrial world's interest in greater democratisation. In 1914 the Ministry of Education proclaimed 'Since our nation is currently adopting a constitutional system, there is no room to doubt that morals should also become constitutional ones. To pursue constitutional duty means to abandon the present authoritarian attitude and to cultivate free and independent spirits'. The third version of the school text on ethics which came out in 1918 included sections on the spirit of enterprise, labour, civic duties, collaboration and public benefit.

Japan's seven centuries of feudalism (the twelfth to the nineteenth century), being so late and so long a period, often underpins twentieth-century attitudes. As Edwin O. Reischauer notes in his book *The Japanese Today* (Tuttle, Tokyo 1988, p.59), 'The political and social organisation of medieval Japan is extremely remote from that of contemporary Japanese society but many of the attitudes developed then, and preserved and reshaped in the later phases of Japanese feudalism, have survived into modern times. Thus the warrior spirit and its sense of values were easily revived by the modern Japanese army, and a strong spirit of loyalty, duty, self-discipline, and self-denial still lingers on from feudal days, shaping the contemporary Japanese personality'. This point was taken up by Professor Kenji Moriguchi over a Sunday meal in Kyoto in March 1989: 'Feudal loyalty permitted a well disciplined workforce. But there was a major difference also in that there was no real Japanese equivalent of Europe's Christianity with its emphasis on *individual* salvation. If you cannot depend on God you must depend on your fellow human beings'.

Eitaro Komatsubara's *Annual Report of the Minister of State for Education* for 1907–08 (Department of Education, Tokyo 1910) catches much of the resulting flavour of educational objectives in the opening 'General Remarks':

It must not be forgotten that if the late war raised Japan to a position of equality with the foremost powers of the world, it also threw her into a labyrinth of international relations which multiplied her responsibilities. If her national life developed from an insular condition into a new one of world-wide importance, the ideas and sentiments of the people at large must have undergone a similar expansion. It is, therefore, high time that the post-bellum measure should be carried out in their completeness with deliberation and foresight, that all legitimate means should be adopted for the full realisation of the national destiny, and that any evils incident to the triumphs of the late war should be completely eliminated. It is beyond question our duty to live simply, avoid display, and continually exhort one another against giving way to indolence. Thus one and all should aim at the full development of the national powers and resources. Every effort should be made to cultivate a good character, sincerity, and candour, and to maintain a high national standard of morality and good-breeding, in order that Japan should advance side-by-side with the foremost powers of the world. Education being a great permanent work undertaken by the state, although the measures and undertakings of today may not produce an immediate result, yet their influence, whether good or otherwise, will tell, in the long run, on the future destiny of the nation.

Having defeated China over the control of Korea in 1894–95, produced in the Anglo-Japanese pact of 1902 the first equal alliance between a Western and non-Western power, and demonstrated that an Asian country could defeat a European in the Russo-Japanese War of 1904–05, Japan might be forgiven a certain smugness in the Minister's words. What is more significant for the direction of education is the listing of broad objectives, in line with 'national destiny'.

From 1930 to 1945 'national destiny' increasingly predominated in the aims of Japanese educational investment. The citizens were frequently reminded of the 'uniqueness' of Japan, which continues as a subtle theme of modern Japan. All countries are unique in their characteristics, but only Japan makes such a cult of the fact. In the Department of Education's *A General Survey of Education in Japan*, published in Tokyo in 1937, it was stated that ' . . . making clear the real import of the culture peculiar to Japan, care is taken to encourage the organisation among pupils and students of moderate research bodies and cultural bodies, special heed being given to proper guidance in the matter'. At this time there was some foreign criticism of what was seen as attempts at thought control in Japanese schools and institutions of higher education. The same document attempted to reassure its international readers:

The Coaching Teacher System: With regard to guidance and training in thought for pupils and students of universities, koto gakko, and special colleges, the work is undertaken chiefly by students' and pupils' superintendents. It is with a view of bringing teachers in general and pupils and students, as the case may be, to closer, more intimate, contact with one another, so that, through the former's personal magnetism and scholastic power, a sound development of the pupils' and students' thought as well as of their intellectual and moral culture may be effectively realised, that this system has been inaugurated. Under the method the whole school is divided into groups of from 20 to 30 pupils or students each, and to each unit is attached a 'coaching' teacher, who is responsible for the direction and moral training of those placed under his leadership, acting as a sort of guarantor for their conduct and behaviour.

As always, the social and political context of such developments does much to explain them. Reischauer suggests (pp.97–8): 'The situation was commonly described as a population problem. The white race had appropriated for itself the lightly inhabited, desirable lands in the Western hemisphere and Australia and was excluding the Japanese from them . . . As the Japanese saw the situation, they were not only being discriminated against in a humiliating way but were also being economically bottled up. The only answer, some felt, was military expansion on the nearby Asian continent'. The Japanese government never seemed in full control of the armed forces and had faced grave opposition in 1930 over the London Naval Treaty. The Mukden Incident of 18 September 1931 was staged by army officers without government approval, but led the military to overrun all of Manchuria and establish Manchukuo in February 1932. Amidst strong nationalistic support in Japan an increasingly ineffective Cabinet found itself back in the imperial business. The League of Nations condemned the Japanese action in Manchuria which led Japan to end its membership.

The beginning of the 1930s was a period of political assassinations. With the murder of a second prime minister by a group of naval officers in May 1932, a naval admiral became premier, with another military man succeeding him in 1934. Despite great success by the political parties in the elections of 1932, 1936 and 1937 the Cabinet was dominated by the military. Young army officers almost took over power when on 26 February 1936 they assassinated members of the government and took control of much of Tokyo. However, the military leadership eventually decided to suppress the rising. This was

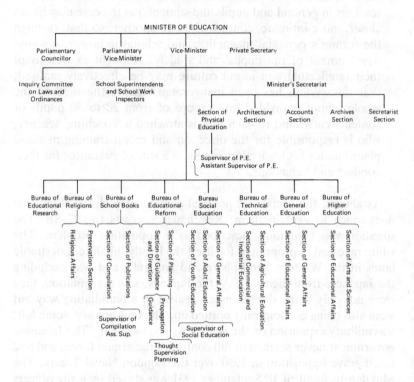

MINISTER OF EDUCATION

Parliamentary Councillor | Parliamentary Vice-Minister | Vice-Minister | Private Secretary

Inquiry Committee on Laws and Ordinances

School Superintendents and School Work Inspectors

Minister's Secretariat

Section of Physical Education | Architecture Section | Accounts Section | Archives Section | Secretarist Section

Supervisor of P.E.
Assistant Supervisor of P.E.

Bureau of Educational Research | Bureau of Religions | Bureau of School Books | Bureau of Educational Reform | Bureau Social Education | Bureau of Technical Education | Bureau of General Edcuation | Bureau of Higher Education

Religious Affairs
Preservation Section
Section of Compilation
Section of Publications
Section of Guidance and Direction
Section of Planning
Section of General Affairs
Section of Adult Education
Section of Youth Education
Section of General Affairs
Section of Commercial and Industrial Education
Section of Agricultural Education
Section of Educational Affairs
Section of General Affairs
Section of Educational Affairs
Section of Arts and Sciences

Supervisor of Compilation
Ass. Sup.

Propagation
Guidance

Supervisor of Social Education

Thought Supervision Planning

FIGURE 4.3 *Japan: Organisation of the Department of Education*

followed by the crushing of disunity within the army and navy,but further loss of power by the parliamentary Diet. In 1937 party participation in the Cabinet ended under an army general premier.

   The establishing of a Bureau of Educational Reform (see Figure 4.3) with responsibility for 'Thought Supervision Planning', whilst unlikely to appeal to Westerners, became more understandable in the light of the violence and relative instability of Japan in the 1930s. It would appeal to a military government launching on an ambitious imperial role in Asia, and particularly in a society where education was recognised as central to shaping the style of citizens. Such confidence in the power of education led to high investment in provision.

The 1937 General Survey opens with the statement, 'In March, 1935 Japan had 46 138 educational institutions. They comprised schools of all kinds, from elementary schools to universities, and had a total enrolment of 14 035 823. These schools were distributed throughout the country on an average of 11 to every 100 square kilometres and the enrolment averaged 20 to every 100 of the population'. No other Asian country in the 1930s had such an impressive provision of education. No other state had greater faith in the power of education to mould men and women.

The Bureau of Educational Reform had been established on 21 July 1937, but was a replacement of the Bureau of Thought Supervision which had as its brief 'affairs connected with the innovation and improvement in education and learning, considered in the light of the fundamental meaning of the national polity'. This had arisen out of the 1929 Bureau of Student Control (for directing and investigating students' thoughts). It is worth pondering just why the most extensively educated nation in Europe (Germany) and the country with the most impressive educational system in Asia (Japan) abandoned democratic politics as the 1930s progressed. Logic would suggest that the higher the general level of education the greater the individual commitment to a democratic form of government. In each instance a peculiar set of circumstances, both within frameworks of economic vulnerability fuelling nationalism, seem to have permitted the emergence of totalitarian regimes.

In the International Society for Educational Information's *The Modernisation of Japanese Education* (Tokyo, 1986), Volume 1 on 'Thought and System' includes a significant review (pp. 37–8) of the problems associated with Japan's education system prior to 1945:

> The first was the promotion of standardisation. As previously mentioned, Japan's modernisation was due to strong government leadership and national guidance. This same characteristic of national guidance became manifest in the important role played by education in the promotion of modernisation. Here, excessive state control was brought to bear on education, from its administration through to the curriculum, accelerating the standardisation of education.
>
> Standardisation was thought ideal to mould the national consciousness. For example, the preparation of textbooks was nationalised. Total loyalty to the state was emphasised, particularly in the ethics and morality course.

TABLE 4.1   *Japan Proper: Statistics of Education*
1 March 1938

Type of School	Schools	Students	Teachers
Elementary Schools	25 906	11 792 738	268 685
Boys' Middle Schools	563	364 486	14 252
Girls' High Schools	996	454 423	16 887
Vocational Schools	1355	477 596	20 877
Youths' Schools	17337	2 041 321	–
Boys' Higher Schools (Koto Gakko) and Preparatory Schools	32[1]	17 017	1 283
Universities	45	72 968	6 385
Colleges (Semmon Gakko)	118	72 088	–
Higher Vocational colleges[2]	61	27 613	2 525
Normal Schools	101	30 783	–
Higher Normal Schools for Men	2	1 805	–
Higher Normal Schools for Women	2	886	–
Special Institutes for Training Teachers	1	58	–
Institute for Training Business School Teachers	3	232	–
Institutes for Training Youth School Teachers	49	1 596	–
Schools for the Blind	78	5 160	–
Schools for the Deaf and Dumb	62	5 870	–
Miscellaneous Schools	1 926	272 140	–
Total	48 637	15 638 780	–
Kindergartens	2 001	162 027	–

1. Of which seven included both lower and higher courses.
2. *Jitsugyo Semmon Gakko.* Incorporated into *Semmon Gakko* as of January 1943.

SOURCE: *Japan Year Book,* 1940–41.

Second, problems arose from the formation of concepts of individuality and individual rights. If a national consciousness was to be created, an individual's sense of his or her own rights and a consciousness of human rights could only be encouraged half-heartedly. Instead of a modern consciousness of human rights, nationalistic patriotism was inculcated, concentrating on the importance of the state. Thus, the result of the policy of strengthening defence and national prosperity was the birth of militarism.

The third problem was the borrowed nature of the knowledge being taught. In promoting the government's policies of modernisation and industrialisation, the policy adopted for the introduction of science and technology was to borrow the knowledge wholesale from the West. The means of propagation of this knowledge did not support its germination into real learning or scientific thinking. An education centred on rote memory and written tests came into existence mainly because the rapid spread of knowledge became an end in itself. This closed the door to the evolution and modernisation of Japan's highly developed and cultivated tradition and enervated its indigenous creative potential.

The fourth problem was the importance attached to written tests. The placing great weight on a person's school record, brought about by closely linking the school system and the mechanism for selecting and developing talented people, greatly intensified entrance exam competition because students were ambitious to obtain higher social positions and higher posts. Education became a matter of just passing exams. Furthermore, since the selection of capable people occurred mainly in the schools, a school-centred view of education was created.

The fifth problem is called the double structure of education. Efficient training courses for a talented élite was differentiated from other courses and, in terms of educational history, a nineteenth-century school system called the 'double-track' system was created. This brought about inequalities in educational opportunity at secondary and higher levels of education.

By 1938 student numbers were approaching 16 million (see Table 4.1) with, inevitably, the vast bulk found in the elementary schools. During the late 1930s and early 1940s Japan's increasing war effort saw nationalism greatly emphasised and the rights of the individual further eroded. In 1941 *The Way of the Imperial Subject* was published, and was from then on found in a majority of schools as a text. Within it the government's wartime philosophy is succinctly stated:

What we call private life is nothing but the practice of the way of the Imperial subject who supports the heavenly throne of the Emperor. As is correctly stated in the Shinto prayer 'from the extremity where the heavenly clouds float to the extremity of the vale where toads wade' the Japanese people live under the domain of the Emperor's rule and therefore are Imperial subjects. Thus, it is not permissible to regard one's private life as subject to one's will and to be indifferent to the nation, and thereby to lead a selfish life. Not even a bowl of food nor a suit of clothes can be regarded as private possessions. Nor is there any private self who is not subject to the nation in play or in sleep. Every one of them is closely related to the nation. Serve the government, attend closely to your trade, parents nurture your children, and children follow your studies; in our nation, all these represent the duties of the people through which they serve the nation according to their abilities. Herein is the meaning of national life in Japan.

Of course, there is a danger in reading such statements within the context of Western cultural experience and not Japanese history. As all commentators on Japan emphasise, there is a greater commitment to 'the group' (variously defined) than to the individual. Extra-family groups (for example, work colleagues) are usually more important than the family. The nuclear family is one group to which the individual belongs, whilst even larger than workplace is the nation itself. Because the group allegiance has such importance the individual works to the best of his or her ability so that it may be successful. Like all societies, Japan is continually changing and more individualistic Japanese may result from economic prosperity, but in 1941 the power of the group made *The Way of the Imperial Subject* less than difficult to absorb into Japanese culture. This is not to suggest that the Japanese, then or now, lacked individuality. They are a people rich in personal characteristics and views, but they seek consensus before action. Strong individual leaders are not normally welcomed, which may be one reason why Japanese labour relations are so much more successful than are the British with their often provocative belief that 'managers must be left to manage'.

By 1941, as Table 4.2 shows, the Japanese elementary school curriculum gave considerable emphasis to Japanese language and history, military training and gymnastics, and the teaching of morals. Science was less evident. As the war in the Pacific became more pressing the Cabinet on 21 December 1943 approved a school reorganisation plan to further meet the economic needs of the country.

The number of students to be admitted to the faculty of literature

(Number of hours per week)

COURSE	SUBJECT		Elementary Course						Higher Course		Total
		I	II	III	IV	V	VI	VII[1]	VIII	
National or Civic Course	Morals	10	11	2	2	2	2	2	2	71
	Japanese Language	-	-	8	8	7	7	4	4	
	Japanese History	-	-	-	-	2	2	2	2	17
	Geography	-	-	-	1	2	2	2	2	
Business and Technical Course		-	-	-	-	-	-	(B) 5 (G) 2	(B) 5 (G) 2	(B) 10 (G) 4
Science and Mathematics Course	Arithmetic	5	5	5	5	5	5	3	3	47
	Science			1	2	2	2	2	2	
Physical Training	Military Training									
	Gymnastics	4	5	4	4	5	5	(B) 6 (G) 5	(B) 6 (G) 4	39 36
Art	Music	-	-	2	2	2	2	1	1	10
	Penmanship	2	2	2	2	1	1	1	1	8
	Drawing work (and/or Domestic Science for girls)			2	2	4	4	2 5	2 5	22 88
	TOTAL NUMBER OF HOURS PER WEEK	21	23	26	30	31	32	(B) 30 (G) 29	(B) 30 (G) 28	(B) 224 (G) 221

(B): Number of hours per week for boys
(G): Number of hours per week for girls

at High Schools is to be reduced to two classes for the First High School, and one class for other High Schools; as for the faculty of science, there are to be eight classes for each of the First to Eighth High Schools, and five classes for each of the other ones; the capacity of government and other public colleges of science is to be expanded; some High Commercial Schools are to be changed into Industrial Colleges and the curriculum of the rest is to be reformed; while private colleges of sciences are to be well organised and expanded, those of literature are to be amalgamated, if possible, and the number of students to be admitted is to be half the present number; as for Imperial Universities and other Government and Public Universities, the full number of students to be admitted to those of science is to be increased, while the College of Commerce shall reduce its enrollment to about one-third of its present number; as for private universities (technical departments included), those of science are to be well organised and expanded as far as possible, but those of literature and their technical departments shall reduce their enrollment of students to one-third and one-half of their present number respectively. Arrangements are to be made to merge or convert those universities as far as possible (reported in US Army Manual M354-15, 23 June 1944).

Like the war-ravaged Germans, the Japanese would, despite all, exit from the Second World War with their most precious asset enhanced, namely their well-educated and science-imbued population. And the Japanese belief in the uniqueness of their society, whilst temporarily bruised, would survive. After the death of Emperor Hirohito Ian Buruma wrote a critical article in the *Observer* of 15 January 1989 which is worth quoting at some length as it gives a contrary view of Japanese history to that favoured by perhaps most scholars, Japanese or foreign:

Peace and the unique national propensity - so it is claimed - for social harmony not only fudge political responsibility, but the propagation of such values often has a political purpose. After the collapse of the authoritarian Tokugawa Government in the middle of the last century, Japan, ruled by an energetic oligarchy of upstart samurai, set out to become a modern state. One thing the new rulers feared more than anything else, more even than conflict abroad, for which they showed a marked taste, was conflict at home. Political pluralism was seen as a threat to the at High Schools is to be reduced to two classes for the First High School, and one class for other High Schools; as for the faculty of science, there are to be eight classes for each of the First to Eighth High Schools, and five classes for each of the other ones; the capacity of government and other public colleges of science is to be expanded; some High Commercial Schools are to be changed into Industrial Colleges and the curriculum of the rest is to be reformed; while private colleges of sciences are to be well organised and expanded, those of literature are to be amalgamated, if possible, and the number of students to be admitted is to be half the present number; as for Imperial Universities and other Government and Public Universities, the full number of students to be admitted to those of science is to be increased, while the College of Commerce shall reduce its enrollment to about one-third of its present number; as for private universities (technical departments included), those of science are to be well organised and expanded as far as possible, but those of literature and their technical departments shall reduce their enrollment of students to one-third and one-half of their present number respectively. Arrangements are to be made to merge or convert those universities as far as possible (reported in US Army Manual M354-15, 23 June 1944).

Like the war-ravaged Germans, the Japanese would, despite all, exit from the Second World War with their most precious asset enhanced, namely their well-educated and science-imbued population. And the Japanese belief in the uniqueness of their society, whilst temporarily bruised, would survive. After the death of Emperor Hirohito Ian Buruma wrote a critical article in the *Observer* of 15 January 1989 which is worth quoting at some length as it gives a contrary view of Japanese history to that favoured by perhaps most scholars, Japanese or foreign:

Peace and the unique national propensity - so it is claimed - for social harmony not only fudge political responsibility, but the propagation of such values often has a political purpose. After the collapse of the authoritarian Tokugawa Government in the middle of the last century, Japan, ruled by an energetic oligarchy of upstart samurai, set out to become a modern state. One thing the new rulers feared more than anything else, more even than conflict abroad, for which they showed a marked taste, was conflict at home. Political pluralism was seen as a threat to the new order and had to be contained, by force if necessary, but more usually through subtle coercion. A mythology was literally created out of a mishmash of modern and archaic forms which, against all historical evidence, ascribed a unique harmony and homogeneity to Japanese culture and society. Conflict was not just socially undesirable, but positively un-Japanese. The Meiji Emperor, brought to Tokyo from his traditional quarters in Kyoto, to serve as a figurehead for the new oligarchy, was made to embody the superiority of the Japanese race - superior because of the purity of the one unbroken imperial bloodline and the unique harmony and homogeneity of Japanese culture as defined by the rulers. Nationalist philosophers extolled the virtues of the family state, where, as the slogan had it, 'one hundred million hearts beat as one'. The will of the Emperor could, in its benevolence, not but be the will of the people. Dissidents were not only un-Japanese, but in danger of committing lese majesté. Politicians and businessmen, regarded as selfish and greedy, were clearly less suited to represent the imperial will than military men and bureaucrats who were above political conflict, though often paralysed by internal strife. Containing conflict on the home front meant that Japanese energies had to be deflected elsewhere, to the new colonies of Formosa, Korea, Manchuria and, later, all the way to Burma. In the rhetoric of the time, all the world had to be brought under one roof to benefit from the divine benevolence of the Emperor...The idea that all Japanese are tied by a spiritual bond of cultural, racial and social harmony, is still widely believed and sometimes innocently, sometimes for political reasons, promoted. Such propaganda, even when prewar blood-and-soil terminology is carefully avoided, helps keep Japanese society closed to outsiders and oppressive to those within. The myth of harmony and consensus is also a useful justification for authoritarian bureaucrats and the ruling Liberal Democratic Party to behave as if they naturally represent the will of the people because of their benevolent stuardship of national harmony. The imperial institution does not inspire enormous enthusiasm among the Japanese people, but that is not its function. It does add symbolic value to the myth of unique national consensus and racial purity.

I have a great liking for Japan and cherish my Japanese friends for their generosity, humanity and reliability, but it is the only country some resentment. The Japanese can easily slip into an inferiority complex regarding the West from which they have had to borrow so much. To repeat again an obvious truth, all dynamic cultures borrow from everywhere. But such healthy practice can produce resentment towards the donor

This is particularly the case with countries which take too seriously their own myths. The problem with people is that myths can be as easily believed as reality. No 'people' are special, but the Japanese have been taught since the nineteenth century that they are. Despite the glory of the world's cultural variety, all of humanity is the same. What we have come to call 'race' is an unhelpful term as all peoples are of a huge variety of physical types. The people of Japan are racially as diverse as those of Britain - the already racially diverse peoples of the South Pacific have been mixed with further immigrations from the racially diverse peoples of North China, the very varied groups of South China and Southeast Asia, Koreans, and a dash of innumerable other physical types from the Ainu to Europeans (from the sixteenth century to today). What the Japanese mythology is mistaking for racial purity is the uniformity of the modern mass culture which has been achieved largely through an impressively uniform educational system. Japan entered the post-1868 era with a remarkable level of social and political cohesion and unity. This had been achieved over many centuries and makes a sharp contrast to, say, such present modernising states as Nigeria with their tribal diversity and obligation, and their main political form resulting only from the former colonial boundaries. Education in modern Japan has always been the primary means of sustaining unity and nationalism.

In achieving conformity the Japanese used their Emperor as a symbol of their country's uniqueness. The Imperial line is supposed to have begun when the British were building Stonehenge, and its 'accepted' history confirms for many Japanese their own distinctiveness. The institution of Emperor has been used ruthlessly since the Tokugawa rule crashed into upstart shouts of, to quote a memorable phrase again, 'Revere the Emperor and Expel the Barbarians'. Since the Restoration the Emperor has often had little power (although he had a great influence in the mid-Meiji era), but has had his name used to justify the implementation of policy. As Tsugio Ajisaka ('Moral Education in Japan', in *Education in Japan*, Volume III, 1968) noted of the Imperial Rescript on Education of 1890:

It became not only the spiritual arm of the Meiji Constitution but also the basic principle of Japanese Education. It was taught that the purpose of all schools was to give common education and training to the students on the basis of the Imperial Rescript on Education, creating a uniform national character through the practice of the imperial doctrine, and attempting to cultivate creative and practical imperial subjects through the training of intelligence and virtue, mind and body.

Up to 1945 (and there is much evidence to suggest also since 1945) there was a consistency in educational objectives. It is useful to compare a little of the content of 24 lectures given by a former Japanese Minister of Education, Baron Dairoku Kikuchi, at London University in 1907 (*Japanese Education*, London: John Murray, 1909) with Articles from the 1941 new Education Regulations. On the Imperial Rescript Kikuchi explained, 'I fear that, however we may translate it, the translation will scarcely convey to you the same message that the original does to a Japanese; in fact, it may be said that our whole moral and civic education consists in so imbuing our children with the spirit of the Rescript that it forms a part of our national life'. Perhaps even more revealing was the Baron's statement on female education, although it is worth reminding ourselves that many of his British audience would have considered Japanese views far from out of the ordinary.

It is our belief that the vocation of a woman is to be wife and mother; we demand it of our women that they shall be good wives and wise mothers as a duty that they have to perform as Japanese subjects, just as we demand of men that they shall perform their duties in various professions and trades and in general as Japanese subjects...Our female education, then, is based upon the assumption that women marry, and that its object is to fit girls to become good wives and wise mothers...The house was, and still is, as I have said before, the unit of society, not the individual...Social conditions cannot change so rapidly as legal enactments or political systems, especially in what concerns women. Such has been the object kept in view in framing the present system of female education - in a word, to fit girls to be good wives and mothers, proper helpmates and worthy companions of the men of the Meiji, and noble mothers to bring up future generations of Japanese.

As the 1893 Ministry of Education 'Outlines of Modern Education in Japan' had announced, 'The culture of the moral sensibilities should be chiefly attended to in the education of children. Hence in teaching any subject of study, special attention should be paid to those topics which are commented with moral education and with education specially adapted to make of the children good members of the community. The knowledge and skill imparted to children should be sound and practical. Therefore such topics as refer to the necessities of daily life and conduct shall be selected and taught, so as to enable the children intelligently and practically to apply what they have learned' (Article 1 of the Regulations Concerning the Elementary Education Course).

Baron Dairoku Kikuchi's views of Japanese women appear to have been accepted until recent times. Professor Makoto Yamaguchi, another friend, now at Ryutsu Keizai University, has given me a copy of her paper *Feminism and Adult Education in Japan* (June 1988) in which she points out, 'One of the peculiarities of women's problems in Japan is that women are unaware of their human individuality. That is because they have for a long time been subjected to the traditional family system, and 'Good Wife and Wise Mother' have been regarded as the description of an ideal woman...It was only since the International Women's Year in 1975 that the Japanese started arguing about the flexibility of sex-roles. In the 1980s people are becoming more aware of sexual equality, as a result of the international influences and equal participation in various fields'.

The 1941 Regulations were to reinforce further such characteristics as those favoured for national unity and conformity. Much was made of 'Kodo' or 'Principles of Imperial Benevolent Rule' to ensure that women were 'Good Wives and Wise Mothers' and men were energetic nationalists. Article 1 contained four important points, namely (1) 'Training in the Kodo shall dominate all educational activities, by fostering the national spirit and strengthening faith in the national polity'. Any middle aged or older Japanese will offer, usually gleefully, to recite from memory the Imperial Rescript as a continuing part of this pre-1945 process. Point (2) stated 'An outline of the Japanese culture shall be impressed on the public with emphasis on salient features. Also the general situation of East Asia in particular and the world in general shall be taught them so as to make them conscious of the position of the Empire'. Again, it is worth reminding British readers of our prewar traditions of giving similar tuition in state schools on the British Empire. Point (3) stressed that 'Mind and body shall be trained as a whole with a view to balanced development of national characteristics'. Point

(4) reminded teachers that 'Festivals, ritual, school programmes, work, athletics, hygiene and other educational measures shall be incorporated into the curriculum...so as fully to realise the real aim of education'. Article 3 directed:

> The national or civic course (kokuminka) is aimed at clarifying the essence of national polity, fostering the national spirit and making pupils conscious of their duties for the Empire, by improving their knowledge of the morals, language, history and geography of Japan. The pupils must be induced to appreciate the happiness of being born in the Empire, they must be trained to live in piety and in devoted service to the public. Pupils must be made to understand that the national spirit is based on the aspiration of the Empire, which is to go on developing forever. Further, they must be taught not only to understand that the history and geography of Japan have fostered a fine national character, but to strive to create and develop the unique culture of Japan. The general situation of East Asia in particular and the world in general must be laid before the pupils in an effort to qualify them as future members of a great nation...

Such an ego-massaging myth as the uniqueness of the Japanese was, and is, the most powerful of incentives to make a maximum contribution, and to conform. Interestingly, Article 4 was an acknowledgement that Western science was essential to economic and military success:

> The science and mathematics course is intended to foster a rational creative spirit, to prepare ground for contributions to the development of the State, by making correct observation of natural phenomena and dealing with them properly in the course of daily life. Pupils must be made to understand that scientific progress offers substantial contribution to the development of the State, and also that they are charged to create new forms of culture in furthering Japan's progress. The pupils must be trained to study mathematics and the laws of nature. A faculty for analytical and logical observation must be fostered, with emphasis on a comprehensive and intuitive grasp of the subject under observation . . . Common sense regarding national defence must be cultivated by drawing attention to the fact that national defence depends a great deal on scientific progress.

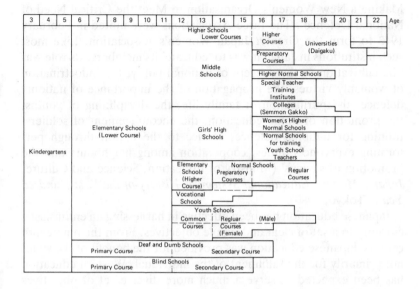

FIGURE 4.4 *The School System in 1945*

Despite such encouragement of science, in 1941 Japan was to attack the United States at Pearl Harbor, although it knew of the latter's scientific and economic superiority. Japanese will power was expected to dominate American economic reality. Although complete and resounding defeat followed four years later, the myth of Japanese uniqueness survived. Article 5 stated: 'The physical course is aimed at coordinating training of both mind and body as a whole for the purpose of building up health and cultivating the spirit of fortitude, manliness and generosity . . . Pupils must be induced to realise that strong and sturdy physique and vigorous spirit are essential for a national defence . . . . . '. Article 6 concluded, 'Military arts in the physical training course shall be cultivated for the purpose of training both body and mind and also of fostering the samurai spirit, by making the pupils acquainted with the elements of those arts'.

In 1901 Okumura Ioko had established the Women's Patriotic Association. The Greater Japan Federation of Women's Groups was founded in 1930. In 1932 came the Greater Japan Women's National Defence Association. Such diversity did not appeal to the government, and in June 1941 the Cabinet established 'Guidelines for

Making a New Women's Organisation to Meet the Critical Need of National Defence'. The three Associations were united in February 1942 to form the Greater Japan Women's Association. Like most such institutions in Japan it was to 'educate' its members. Its role was 'the cultivation of the concept of national polity, the indoctrination of womanly virtues, the propagation of the importance of national defence, the purification of family life, the disciplining of youths, the promotion of home education, the encouragement of soldiers, training for national defence, service to the nation through performing everyone's duties, cooperation among neighbours and the promotion of savings' (Ministry of Education, Science and Culture, *Japan's Modern Educational System: A History of the First Hundred Years*, Tokyo, 1980).

Japanese education has been effective in harnessing an enthusiastic citizenry to a set of clear and simple objectives. From the nineteenth century Japanese education was provided for the benefit of the state, not primarily for the fulfilment of the individual. Western education has been expected to serve a much more diverse set of objectives and is thus judged at present less successful because the movement to the right in politics which came in the 1970s has made economic growth the only criteria. Japan has been remarkably impressive in its material development, and little has been more important to that success than its education system, except easy access to Western innovation. As the Ministry of Education stated in 1963 (*Japan's Growth and Education*): 'A considerable part of the increase in national income caused by improved human capabilities is attributable to the increased level of education of the labour force . . . it is estimated that the increase of educational capital contributed 25 per cent of the increase in the national income of Japan in the 25 years from 1930 to 1955'. I suspect the contribution has been greater since the 1950s if only because the economy's needs have become more complex and demanding. The need for 'brain workers' has long overtaken the economy's requirement for human muscle.

In his book *Burakumin: A Japanese Minority and Education* (The Hague: Martinus Nijhoff, 1971) N. Shimahara concluded that ' . . . the heart of prejudice has dissolved little'. It is worth repeating that the general level of education in Japan is probably the world's highest, but it is an educational system which encourages destructive human myths such as the Japanese as a racially pure, special people. This doubtlessly fuels Japanese economic determination, but also racism, arrogance, and the familiar British malady of Little

Englanders. Japan is making many efforts to overcome the country's desire to concentrate only on its own affairs and to ignore the rest of the world.

In our many discussions Professor Takamichi Uesugi has used the phrase 'Japan needs to be a cultural, not economic, powerhouse'. That will be difficult as it means a great change of emphasis in the educational system. The period from 1930 to 1945 highlighted the strengths and weaknesses of the approach to educational provision as laid down after the Meiji Restoration. As we shall see, from 1945 there were major efforts to bring about change but Shimahara is one of many writers who recognise: 'There was a marked transformation of the roles of the schools which occurred around 1952. These changes were indicative of the inception of the phase of reaction. In the period of reaction and stabilisation, the schools have become agents for intellectual conditioning . . . . Two new laws were enacted in 1956 which aimed at the concentration of power in the national government'. This was a return to the familiar model of Japanese education with almost total central government authority, very high overall performance from the students and staff, a limited number of clear national objectives related to the needs of the economy, and political stability along conservative lines. It has given Japan huge economic successs and well-read citizens. The only time I have ever looked at the television and radio page of a Japanese newspaper (in 1989) it began, 'Today's Choice: Elevators are an indispensable part of high-rise buildings, but most people don't know how they work . . . ' The Japanese take their learning seriously, and would shame the often ill-informed British citizen. But the educational system perhaps needs to aim for a questioning citizen. In the light of its overwhelming economic and social stability this may seem unimportant to Japan. However, I remain uneasy that the proposed changes in the school curriculum which are due to be implemented in 1992–94 will give further emphasis to certain less than healthy characteristics of Japanese education which can be summed up as 'nationalism'. They are to further instil 'a sense of Japanese identity', stress 'veneration of the Emperor', and patriotism. It will become mandatory to raise the national flag (the Sun Flag) and sing the national anthem (Kimigayo Anthem) at each ceremony, both of which are closely associated with the military regimes of the 1930s and 1940s. The Kimigayo Anthem is in praise of the Emperor. In one of those statements which mystify foreigners Education Minister Takeo Nishioka said of the changes, 'Cries that we are moving backward are outdated. If Japanese children do not respect their flag and their anthem it is offensive to other countries'. Schoolteachers who do not comply with the order to raise the flag or sing the anthem will face their pay being stopped or promotion blocked. In continuing moves to more firmly re-establish the continuity of Japan's 120 years of Meiji Restoration-inspired educational provision greater emphasis will be given to themes such as love of nation, and it will be permitted to study war heroes such as Admiral Heihachiro Togo, a leader against the Russians at the beginning of the century.

Japan's educational system is very professional and highly effective. In any society education is deeply influential, but none more so than Japan's. It is therefore critically important that there is a full debate between citizens, professional educationalists and central government. Such a debate was not notable in the 1930s. Japan's tradition established in the 1930s of overwhelming central government power is unhealthy. Despite often being filled with officials of remarkably enlightened ideals, the Ministry of Education, Science and Culture (Monbusho) has a long history of ignoring the views and opinions of professional educationalists. It is a characteristic increasingly found in the Department of Education and Science in London as the non-debate over the 1988 Education Reform Act displayed. Such intellectual isolation usually leads to legislative limitations. The period from 1930 to 1945 was a disaster for Japan, and yet the tragedy was partly fuelled by an accommodating educational system inspired and dominated by a central government of eccentric policy.

In a democracy such as Japan it is unfortunate that local influence over educational policy is so modest. Until Thatcherite centralising policies were introduced after 1979 British education, for all its other failures, had as its great strength the ability of local citizens to have some say in educational provision which was largely financed and administered through the local education authority. Central governments never like such healthy democratic traditions, which are untidy to the bureaucrat and inhibit a minister's desire for the implementing of grand policy. Locally provided and determined education can also lead to inequalities between different areas. This is the cost of achieving a rich variety of provision and local control. Without a doubt the Japanese tradition of central government authority with attendant high investment in most areas of education has provided a substantially higher level of education amongst the citizenry. Democracy can be less efficient.

Toshiko Fujita, the wife of Professor Hideo Fujita of Rissho University, was born in the early 1930s. Thus her early school education was gained during the period of Japanese militarism. The Fujita's beautiful house overlooking the sea challenges the ill-mannered European claim that the Japanese live in rabbit hutches. What startles the British visitor the most is not the superb view, but certain items of interior decoration. Toshiko Fujita, despite the efforts of Japan's central government of the 1930s and early 1940s, is a student and fan of Beatrix Potter. It is difficult to use the writings of Beatrix Potter to reinforce Japanese militarism or to stress Japanese uniqueness. The house is full of Peter Rabbit posters and Beatrix Potter books. As we all come to another country needing to modify our assumptions, I asked what had led to her interest in these very English stories. She had been introduced to Peter Rabbit by her mother when she was three. After that she had relished the stories as 'a world of imagination', with insights into such familiar themes as that of the relationship between mother, father and child. Within the educational system's achievement of a high level of social conformity in a comprehensively literate and numerate population there are reassuring mavericks. How the Japanese militarists during the period of Imperial expansion and Emperor worship of the 1930s would have coped with the undermining implications of well-read mothers introducing their daughters to Peter Rabbit is difficult to say. What is notable is that it happened.

The Bureau of General Business of the Department of Education in 1884 prepared 'General Outlines of Education' for Japan's participation in the International Health Exhibition in London in 1884. It is a very factual pamphlet revealing nothing of the continuing debates over control and direction of Japanese education taking place in Tokyo. It does reveal, as do all such nineteenth-century documents, the high degree of central government control using a mythical authority of the Emperor which later permitted the military in the 1930s and 1940s to highjack the state:

All the administrative affairs of the country are under the control of the Emperor. Under Daijôkwan or Privy Council, there are ten departments, viz., the Departments of Foreign Affairs, Interior, Finance, War, Marine, Education, Agriculture and Commerce, Public Works, Justice, and the Imperial Household, and also the Senate, and the Supreme Court of Judicature. These all form part of the administration of the country. There is a governor in each

Fu and Ken, who exercises jurisdiction in accordance with the laws and regulations passed by the government, and in conformity with the directions of the various Ministers. In every Gun or Ku, the subdivision of Fu and Ken, there is a Gunchô or Kuchô, who controls that Gun or Ku under the superintendence of the governor, and in conformity with his directions. In a ward or village, there is a Kochô, who, under the supervision of Gunchô or Kuchô, takes charge of the administrative affairs in his jurisdiction. In regard to education, there are school committees specially organised in wards or villages to conduct the various matters concerning the school attendance of children, the establishment and maintenance of schools, and so on, under the supervision of the governor. They are nominated in each school district by the people of that district, and then the governor selects a certain number of those thus nominated. The tenure of office of the school committees is not less than four years, and fixed according to circumstances. Their number, salaries, and the like are determined by the ward or village assembly with the approval of the governor. In case any committee man is incapable of discharging his duty after he has been appointed, the governor causes another nomination to be made. Persons qualified to serve as members of School Committees, or to take part in the nomination of the same, must be males, upwards of 20 years of age, possessing either lands or buildings, and having both legal and actual residence within their respective school districts. The Kochô takes part in the business of school committees in his own school districts. When several wards or villages unite together and establish such schools as professional schools, middle schools, and so on, independent of the limit of the school district in which elementary schools are organised, they nominate special school committees within the limit of the school district thus formed. The regulation as to the mode of nomination, appointment, functions, and the like, are the same as those adopted in the case of school committees of school districts. The Department of Education is one of the ten Departments and the Minister of Education has control over all affairs connected with the education of the country, and with respect to these affairs, he superintends the governors of Fu and Ken.

Those who had seized political power in the Restoration were not democrats. However, under the 1889 Constitution a partly-elected Diet was established to gain further popular support, gratify some of the Western powers, and to relieve political discontent. The organisation of education as revealed by the 1884 document showed some similar regard for local opinion. In 1878 there had been prefectural assemblies, with more local political assemblies following in the 1880s. But such forums had very little power, and by 1890 only 1.26 per cent could vote in Diet elections. However, it is important for the British to recall how many centuries passed before universal male suffrage was achieved in 1867. As M.E. Burton noted in 1914 (*The Education of Women in Japan*, New York: Revell): 'The world has seldom seen so remarkable a transformation as that caused by Commodore Perry's insistent knock upon the closed door of Japan. A mediaeval nation, isolated, feudalistic, and unprogressive, suddenly threw open its doors to international intercourse, established a constitutional monarchy, and set itself to achieve universal education and equality before the law for all citizens'. In such rapid change more of the past survives than is superficially noted. Authoritarian government continues to appeal to traditionalists, even if the authority is the ruling group, not a powerful individual. As Reischauer has written, 'At first, the genro (elder statesmen) were in ultimate control, though not as fully as they had expected to be. By the 1920s the Diet and the parties were at the centre of the balance, and both big business and the general public had increased in power through their influence over the parties. In the 1930s the military, particularly the army, achieved the leading role in the balance and on the eve of the attack on the United States in 1941 concentrated greater power in the hands of General Tojo than any individual had enjoyed for half a century. But even Tojo's authority was that of a group leader, not a dictator, and, when in 1944 the war was seen to be going badly, he meekly left office'.

Mr Saito, who until recently was in charge of the key Life-Long Learning Bureau of the Ministry of Education, Science and Culture could have been a Whitehall mandarin. He was elegant, entertaining, held lightly but enjoyed his obvious power, and said he could see me for half an hour. With a typical civil servant's inbred courtesy he gave me much more time and I took the decision to exit for fear of disrupting his schedule even further. Whilst the Japanese cannily emphasised elementary education provision when they began modernising their country, and have produced through education a much less class-ridden society than Britain, their élite is similar in outward characteristics to that of Western Europe or North America. Mr Saito was dapper.

With my mind full of themes related to the Japanese education system's encouragement of conformity, and doubtful whether the lessons of 1930 to 1945 had been learned, Mr Saito came like a breath of the proverbial fresh air. I left regretting the poor state of cooperation between the Ministry and the professional education-alists, as they have much to learn from each other and effective policy change will demand a partnership. Were civil servants in the 1930s talking as Mr Saito did, or was he, despite his mannerisms and outward appearance, a member of a new breed? Whilst I would expect him to commend education as a life-long experience, as that was his departmental responsibility, I did not anticipate him describing the much admired Japanese schools as 'oppressive', or his telling me that many businessmen, whom the educational system often seems largely designed to benefit, were anxious to change the image of a Japan obsessed with economic success. They dislike the Japanese being labelled 'economic animals'. He felt that the Japanese had an exceptional amount of respect for schools, and after a moment's reflection added 'the schools are too respected'. He hoped his Division would help overcome a school system which was too rigid, and counter the fanatic competition for the top university places. 'How do you change 131 years of job-related education?' was raised by him as a theme, and he made much of the need to have a liberal education system which would enable the Japanese to lead fuller lives. This would entail practical changes like more mature students in universities (now only 1 per cent of the student body), the development of the adult liberal education tradition in institutions such as universities (something of substantial provision in English universities, but now being dismantled) and elsewhere, and a budget change where now over 90 per cent of expenditure was employed on schools. Education was seen as uncoordinated with little cooperation between the schools, social education or the training fields. The Social Education Law was not satisfactory with too much stress on material aid and little on information giving. The local councils of social education had been too prescribed with, for example, schoolteachers suggested as members, where a more widely recruited council with broader-based knowledge might be of greater effectiveness.

In one of our conversations Professor Takamichi Uesugi had said, 'My father knew how to use his leisure time, the next generation has been too busy overworking to increase economic power. There is now a need to stress such things as artistic interests. But we have a non-vocational tradition but not one of liberal adult education like Britain. Alas, we Japanese have to *feel* leisure by going abroad, by spending money, by taking photographs'. Mr Saito represents a feeling in the general public that Japan should now see change in society to reflect economic success and resulting changing expectations. But, as in the 1930 to 1945 period, or most others since Japan was first united under a single administration, the initiatives for change are coming from the top. Michael White of the *Guardian* reported in the 24 February 1989 edition of that newspaper, 'More intriguing however is Japan's domestic model for the twenty-first century. Are the Japanese becoming more individualistic like us and our 'mature' post-industrial societies, more 'internationally compatible' as their sociologists contend? Or does their top-down 'control society' with its manipulated consensus – Big Brother with a smile and a VCR – offer Mrs Thatcher and (Secretary of State for Education and Science) Ken Baker a blueprint?' When I left Mr Saito's office it did seem ironic that the British government in its search for greater economic success should be abandoning a more liberal educational system for a style of economy-obsessed provision it thinks Japan has, whilst the Japanese are seeking an education model not too unlike that which Britain is moving from whilst trying to stress economic development. One of the greatest government reports in British, and possibly world, history was that of the Ministry of Reconstruction in the field of adult education published after the First World War. This is known as The 1919 Report and deeply influenced many countries with its coherent vision of life-long education (a term it used) for citizens, a liberal curriculum, and a careful balancing of the needs of the individual and those of society as a whole. Whereas Britain is returning to a more primitive early Industrial Revolution style of education, Japan may fulfil the ambitious vision of The 1919 Report, but with the lead taken, as ever, by the government. And like many governments, it at times lacks consistency, wanting to develop Japanese education whilst not ceasing its education as part of the economy model. In her authoritative book *The Japanese Challenge* (Tokyo: Kodansha, 1987) Merry White of Harvard suggests, 'Japanese nostalgia sometimes takes in prewar nationalism, because the reformers were raised in the prewar period that forms the point of reference. And some of the fervor they now find missing was indeed related to military mobilization – a fervor which they felt, but may not have understood, as children. Even those old enough to understand that they, too, were part of a war effort were later to remember more the feeling of engagement, and less the rhetoric and nationalistic propaganda that moved adults at the time'.

Professor Kazuyo Yamamoto sang me a song she had learnt at school during the war years, 'Monday, Monday, Tuesday, Wednesday, Thursday, Friday, Friday'. It was originally a Navy song and means for the Japanese sailor a seven-day working week as Sunday becomes another Monday, and Saturday another Friday. The years of military government confirmed that life in Japan was mainly about working for the benefit of the state. Inevitably this meant an education system which supported that purpose. If it was successful, and the Japanese tend to be good at making this successful, then there was bound to be a danger of too much conformity. As a result Education always receives some 10 per cent of the government's total budget. Higher education is notably underfunded, but other areas of the system do well. Unlike the 1930s and early 1940s, the debate about educational objectives is now more open and acceptance of the nineteenth-century view of what education's purposes are much less guaranteed.

In a paper for the Carnegie Foundation for the Advancement of Teaching in 1975 Japanese Minister of Education, Science and Culture Michio Nagai (*An Owl Before Dusk*, Berkeley), writing for an American audience, having received much of his higher education in the US, made two significant points about the history and direction of Japanese education. The first was about producing innovators from the system: 'Dr Henry Dyer, a British scholar who taught at the Engineering College of Tokyo University in the 1870s, told his students that they should try to imitate the West for some years to come, even if they were deeply interested in creation, because the development of Japan at that stage made imitation necessary. Interestingly enough such thinking has been maintained to the present'. Whilst Japan has such excellent access to the expensively acquired innovations of America and Western Europe there is little incentive to change that way of thinking. It makes good economic sense to allow others to sustain such huge investment in creativity. Of course, it does add another vulnerability to a people who see themselves beset by dangers on all sides. This is a traditional view amongst the Japanese who until the latter part of the last century were 80 per cent rural-living where there was a shortage of land, floods, typhoons, earthquakes, fires, and an erratic climate. Industrial and commercial Japan finds the same outlook sustained by its vulnerability due to few natural resources within the country (other than its highly educated workforce), a reliance on a small number of large markets for its exports and their growing hostility (for example, America takes some 30 per cent of all Japanese exports) or, as in the European Economic Community and its plans for 1992, increasing protectionist legislation, its uncompetitive labour costs when facing such rivals as South Korea, Taiwan, Hong Kong and Singapore, and its continuing fear of cultural swamping by the West (thus the reaction of claiming that the Japanese are unique). What if the West should cut it off from its new developments (which Japan then perfects uniquely well?) There are increasing efforts to abandon Dr Henry Dyer's legacy of imitation.

The second point made by Michio Nagai demonstrates just how well over the past 120 years the education system has 'fitted-in'. 'Not only is it true that a business enterprise acts like a large family, but a school also tends to take on the characteristics of an enclosed society. In addition, all these schools and enterprises are ranked into a class order within the total social system. Under such arrangements, each enterprise is forced to compete with other enterprises (and each school with other schools) as a family unit'.

Up until 1932 the Japanese Education Budget had always been larger than the Military Budget. It is easy to see why. Not only were citizens unusually committed to education, but the products of the schools were well suited to the governments' plans for the country. The one weak point of the education system, as viewed from the Cabinet, has always been the universities. They were always more likely to be unpredictable than the carefully regulated schools. This explains the indifference to higher education of recent postwar governments. Getting into first ranking universities is what matters since that means that your son, and sometimes your daughter, is guaranteed a top job. Except for certain areas of professional training what happens in the four years of university education appears to be of less importance. Parents are keen on university education if only to enhance their children's career prospects, but government funding suggests that the Cabinet continues to view higher education suspiciously as less under effective government control than schools.

It is in the field of social education in the 1930s that so many of the continuing characteristics of Japan and its education system are well illustrated. Initially the Department of Education used the term Popular Education to cover such activities as museums, adult education and libraries. The 1887 Regulations of the Department of Education used such words, but in 1921 the Department began employing social education which had been favoured earlier by certain writers. In 1924 a unit on social education was established in the Bureau of General Education, and in 1929 the Bureau of Social Education was set up. It was one of seven such departments of the Ministry of Education, and was subdivided into Youth Education, General Affairs and Adult Education. By the 1930s there were over a hundred directors of social education, and more than two hundred assistant directors in the prefectures. The social education committees had more than 90 000 members. The Department of Education's 1937 Report on Social Education in Japan stated, 'Under the various influences of unrest and instability in the fields of thought and economy, as well as in society throughout the world, Japan is in a so-called "precarious situation". To overcome such a difficult situation it is most necessary for us to arouse the national self-consciousness and foster the spirit of steadfastly resisting such national dangers. In such a situation as this we have to make greater efforts in school education, and aim especially at the promotion of social education, and look forward with hope to favourable results'.

A tight control of a diverse range of activities was the aim of the Bureau of Social Education. Its 'Section of Youths' Education' took charge of Young Men's Associations, Boy Scouts, Youths' Schools, Institutes for Training Teachers of Youths' Schools, National Grants for the Expense of Youths' Education, Investigation of Educational Standards of Those Young Men of Military Age, and any other matters related to the education of young people. The 'Section of General Affairs' looked after Cinema Films, Popular Amusements, Recognition and Recommendation of Good Books, Improvement in Living Conditions, Affairs Concerning Juridical Persons, plus anything else not handled by the other two Sections. The Section of Adult Education was responsible for Adult Education, Libraries, Museums and Other Visual Education Provisions and Social Education Organisations. The Department's 1937 Report illustrates in many ways the tight control the ministry has always exercised in most areas of education. Courses promoted in Adult Education are described as 'to make them sound members of the nation', to pay 'a great deal of attention to the fostering of national belief', 'to enable them to adapt themselves to the trend of the times and to be diligent in the fulfillment of their duties'. The first national library was established in 1872 and in 1899 regulations were passed to encourage local libraries, but the Japanese were to be guided in their reading: 'Recognising books is a system of giving recognition to a book which is acknowledged by the Department of Education as one which is wholesome for social education in answer to the application of the publisher or author . . . On the other hand, recommendation, as distinct from recognition, is given to a book which is especially excellent among those books found to be beneficial to the public in social education, without waiting for the application from the publisher or author'. The objective in workers' education was to 'train workers as sound nationals and good citizens, as well as excellent industrial men', for which in 1935 the Department of Education set up the Central Association of Workers' Education. Of course, it must be remembered that the British government has been tempted to shape the direction of independent educational organisations and institutions from time to time by the judicious allocation of finance. The Central Association of Workers' Education was launched with an annual government subsidy of 150 000 yen. Women's courses run by the Department of Education included courses of study for mothers, 'In order to elevate the character of mothers who take charge of the important duties of the home and to foster their just and rightful views'. Under national control 2500 organisations for social enlightenment were in being aiming at 'the moral advancement of national life' and undertaking 'to foster thoughts among the people and attempt to improve social life'. The cinema was rightly seen as a powerful medium and the Department of Education gave official recognition 'to those films which are found to be proper'. On amusements in general the Report stated, 'It is, therefore, of considerable importance in social education that we should effect an improvement in general entertainments and aim at their sound development, thereby promoting the culture and taste of the masses of people, so that we might contribute to the establishment of a harmonious society'.

The period from 1930 to 1945 was not an abberation in Japanese educational history, but the international crisis emphasised certain characteristics which continue. Education was for the benefit of the state, not primarily for the individual. The aim always was to achieve a 'harmonious society'. Allegiance was to the group and the nation and the symbol of the Emperor was employed to achieve that commitment. The sheer dottiness of Japanese foreign policy in 1941 should not obscure the continuity in government-shaped and led education policy from the 1870s to the present day. In government terms that policy is, and was, a great success. The Potsdam Declaration of 26 July 1945 by America, Britain and the Soviet Union stated, 'The

Japanese Government shall remove all obstacles to the revival and strengthening of democratic tendencies among the Japanese people. Freedom of speech, or religion, and of thought, as well as respect for fundamental human rights, shall be established'. A character in Malcolm Lowry's masterpiece 'Under the Volcano', which was first published in 1947, says in despair, 'Christ Jesus why may we not be simple, why may we not all be brothers?' Both statements caught the flavour at the end of the 1930 to 1945 period.

The United States dropped a first atomic bomb of Hiroshima on 6 August 1945 and a second on Nagasaki on 9 August. On 14 August Japan accepted unconditional surrender. American troops arrived in Japan on 2 September 1945.

5 The American Occupation of Japan

As the Japanese would be the first to admit, it was their good fortune in the Second World War to be largely defeated by the Americans so that the Occupation was an American affair. A Soviet occupation, as Eastern Europe displayed, was a rougher matter. One by Britain would have been similar to that of the American, but London had other priorities and was materially overstretched and massively out-classed by American power.

General Douglas MacArthur, with the title of Supreme Comman-der for the Allied Powers (SCAP), came into his satrap like Lord Curzon taking over as Viceroy of India. He was theatrical, but effective. Despite an Allied Council for Japan being established in Tokyo and a Far Eastern Commission of the allied powers in Washington, the United States was in total control.

Japan had been devastated and American aid was needed to keep it afloat. Almost seven million Japanese troops and settlers were returned from abroad to add to the crisis. However, what SCAP inherited was a remarkably cooperative, disciplined, and, above all else, well-educated people willing to follow American leadership in the light of their emphatic defeat. In response America provided material aid, inspiring leadership from MacArthur, much expertise, and an army of occupation which displayed the best American qualities of good-will to a former enemy, idealism, and a sense of fair play. Whilst it is doubtful whether American initiatives during the Occupation had as much impact on Japanese education as was thought in the 1950s, the benevolent rule of SCAP provided the foundation for Japan's rapid economic recovery. A peace treaty between the United States and Japan was signed in September 1951 and implemented in March 1952. As is reported in *Japan's Growth and Education* (1963), 'After the Second World War the stock of physical capital had recovered to the pre-war level by around 1955 . . . The stock of educational capital in 1960 is twenty three times of that in 1905'. The distinguished historian Hideo Satow, Director of Research Department 1 at Japan's National Institute for Educational Research, pointed out to me that there were some six million Occupation documents already collected. Such a treasure house will excite future generations of academics, but the strategic ones are already well known and frequently used. I am also grateful for the advice of Ichikawa Shogo, Director of Research Department 2 at the Institute, for his advice. We had met in Britain in 1979 for the first time when he was part of a government review of Lifelong Education in Britain, France, Sweden, the United States and West Germany.

In talking of the Occupation when he was a boy Professor Takamichi Uesugi said, 'In 1919 and 1920 education was expanded under government encouragement. Education was democratically inclined. After 1945 many wanted to return to the style of the 1919–20 period. Thus there was sympathy for American aspirations. There was opposition to an American model, but most wanted an increase in schools and a more democratic system. The opposition wanted change to be slower. The major problem for educational expansion was financial. For example, new junior high schools had to be created, the Japanese secondary system changed from a European model to an American model. Many sympathised with the banishing of an élitist system. After the Second World War most Japanese decided to construct a cultural nation, not a military state, so there was great interest in education. After the 1950s the conservative government tried to counter radical change and to reintroduce the former educational system, but could have little success as the bulk of the Japanese liked the newer system. The conservative government continues to worry that the Japanese will lose national spirit, so they continue to stress nationalism to cement the cohesion of the nation. Government policy was influenced by American priorities, for instance, in the rearming of Japan. In order ot have military power the government found it needed nationalism. The Korean War, which broke out in 1950, influenced that policy. The conservative government has kept such a policy since the 1950s. Former Premier Nakasone stressed the importance of nationalism in education and tried to introduce moral education to enhance the national spirit'.

The frame of mind that the Americans brought with them in September of 1945 can be summed up in the two words 'demilitarisation' and, above all else, 'democratisation'. Section 15 of US Army Forces Manual M354–15 of 23 June 1944 opens with the words, 'Japan's Department of Education is important for civil affairs administration because: (a) it guides the principal activity of nearly 16 million students, some four hundred thousand teachers, and about one hundred and ninety thousand priests and controls in the school system the principal means of indoctrination, not only of Japan's intense nationalism, but also of civil obedience; (b) The school system has been organised to train men for Japanese political and economic administration and will need to be readjusted if it is to train personnel for a different post-occupation system; (c) Scientific institutions under the control of the Department undoubtedly hold technical secrets of military importance which should be known to the occupying authorities; (d) The Department of Education enforces religious laws which may need to be modified and controls religious organizations which may need supervision; (e) The facilities controlled by the Department of Education provide effective means of making occupation policies understood by the Japanese'.

Although the anticipated ardent Japanese nationalism and fanaticism seemed not to be there when the Americans began administering the country in the autumn of 1945, predictably, and on behalf of the Supreme Commander for the Allied Powers, Assistant Adjutant General Colonel E.W. Allen on 22 October 1945 issued a Memorandum on the Administration of the Educational System of Japan to the Imperial Japanese Government. The Americans had been in the country for less than two months but they had thought much about their policy priorities before arriving. The Memorandum was an important indication of their concluding views:

1. In order that the newly formed Cabinet of the Imperial Japanese Government shall be fully informed of the objectives and policies of the occupation with regard to Education, it is hereby directed that:

a. The content of all instruction will be critically examined, revised, and controlled in accordance with the following policies: (1) Dissemination of militaristic and ultra-nationalistic ideology will be prohibited and all military education and drill will be discontinued. (2) Inculcation of concepts and establishment of practices in harmony with representative government, international peace, the dignity of the individual, and such fundamental human rights as the freedom of assembly, speech, and religion, will be encouraged.

b. The personnel of all educational institutions will be investigated, approved or removed, reinstated, appointed, reorientated, and supervised in accordance with the following policies: (1) Teachers and educational officials will be examined as rapidly as possible and all career military personnel, persons who have been active exponents of militarism and ultra-nationalism, and those actively antagonistic to the policies of the occupation will be removed. (2) Teachers and educational officials who have been dismissed, suspended, or forced to resign for liberal or anti-militaristic opinions or activities, will be declared immediately eligible for and if properly qualified will be given preference in reappointment. (3) Discrimination against any student, teacher, or educational official on grounds of race, nationality, creed, political opinion, or social position, will be prohibited and immediate steps will be taken to correct inequities which have resulted from such discrimination. (4) Students, teachers, and educational officials will be encouraged to evaluate critically and intelligently the content of instruction and will be permitted to engage in free and unrestricted discussion of issues involving political, civil, and religious liberties.

(5) Students, teachers, educational officials, and public will be informed of the objectives and policies of the occupation, of the theory and practices of representative government, and of the part played by militaristic leaders, their active collaborators, and those who by passive acquiescence committed the nation to war with the inevitable result of defeat, distress, and the present deplorable state of the Japanese people.

c. The instrumentalities of educational processes will be critically examined, revised, and controlled in accordance with the following policies: (1) Existing curricula, textbooks, teaching manuals, and instructional materials, the use of which is temporarily permitted on an emergency basis, will be examined as rapidly as possible and those portions designed to promote a militaristic or ultra-nationalistic ideology will be eliminated. (2) New curricula, textbooks, teaching manuals, and instructional materials designed to produce an educated, peaceful, and responsible citizenry will be prepared and will be substituted for existing materials as rapidly as possible. (3) A normally operating educational system will be re-established as rapidly as possible, but where limited facilities exist preference will be given to elementary education and teacher training.

2. The Japanese Ministry of Education will establish and maintain adequate liaison with the appropriate staff section of the Office of the Supreme Commander for the Allied Powers, and upon request

will submit reports describing in detail all action taken to comply with the provision of this directive.

3. All officials and subordinates of the Japanese Government affected by the terms of this directive, and all teachers and school officials, both public and private, will be held personally accountable for compliance with the spirit as well as the letter of the policies enunciated in this directive.

Such determined American policy had some impact on the shape of postwar Japanese society. Whilst Japan remains a country of hierarchies, American belief in striving for a classless society has had greater success than in the United States itself. As will be repeated, Japan is much closer to the egalitarian mass society, with fewer extremes of poverty and wealth by far than in America. Education has been of paramount importance in achieving a more equal society since 1945. It has also aided political stability, although not necessarily promoted a vigorous pursuit of democracy. The latter in Japan works to different rules from those familiar to the West. Since the 1950s politics have been dominated by the Liberal Democratic Party which resulted from an amalgamation of the Liberal and Democratic Parties (which had their roots in the first political parties of Itagaki in 1874 and Okuma in 1882) in 1955. Normally the Liberal Democratic Party contains perhaps five major factions. A Diet member almost invariably belongs to one of the factions. This comes within the Japanese tradition of group membership which was bound to make the results of American efforts to firmly establish democracy in Japan somewhat different from the political systems of the West.

In December of 1945 the All Japan Teachers' Union and the Japan Educators' Union were created. On 4 December the Ministry of Education published *A New General Plan of Female Education Reform* which proclaimed: 'We intend to reform female education with a view to giving equal opportunity of receiving education to men and women; raising female education to the level of men's education, and furthering mutual respect among men and women'. Over the last 45 years this good intention has had less impact than the Americans and their Mombusho allies desired. To quote again a conversation with Professor Takamichi Uesugi:

There are large male and female differences in the educational system. For example, although numbers of women are increasing, four year university courses are overwhelmingly male in students, whilst the two year junior college courses are ninety per cent female. Junior colleges have tended to be looked upon as finishing schools. In 1975 Women's Year saw central and local government beginning to accept women's liberation, but the magnificent National Women's Education Centre (opened in Saitama Prefecture in 1977 as part of the Japanese government's plan of action for the United Nations Decade for Women launched in 1975) would not be necessary if women's status were higher. The traditional attitude to women is still present, despite such legislation as that of 1986 which outlawed sex discrimination. Many Japanese companies still want the wife to be a housewife to provide a support for their hardworking employee.

An invitation by the Supreme Commander for the Allied Powers brought an American Education Mission to Japan in 1946. To prepare them for their visit SCAP compiled a handbook entitled *Education in Japan*. It was put together from various sources, including work done by education officers throughout the country, by the Civil Information and Education Section and dated 15 February 1946. Again, the flavour of the American attitude can be gained from a selection of quotations: 'Beginning about 1931, intensified in 1937, and culminated in 1941, Japanese educational aims rejected the virtues and adopted the evils of civic obedience and Imperial loyalty. The emphasis on militaristic nationalism was characterized by: (i) Total subservience of the individual to the state; (ii) Consciousness of the divine mission of Japan in Asia and in the world; (iii) Admiration of and proficiency in the military arts' (p.8.). 'From their inception, the purpose of normal schools has been to 'train' individuals in loyalty to the Emperor, love of country, and obedience to authority so that they would become models for their pupils to emulate. The policy, "to lead men to righteousness is far more important than to make them learned . . . ", has been reflected in the intellectual sterility of the normal schools' (p.26). 'The education system was utilized by the Japanese as the most important single means for conditioning the people to an acceptance of a Shinto centered state' (p.31). 'The Ministry of Education has compiled, edited, and supervised the publication of all national textbooks (approximately two hundred and fifty), teachers' manuals, and teaching materials . . . ' (p.32). 'In April 1938 attendance at youth schools, which were part-time continuation schools, and membership of the Youth Corps were made compulsory' (p.41). As is usually the case in such writings, the style of the handbook says as much about American attitudes and education as about that of Japan. As always it is worth stressing further that those things which Japan accepted from the imposed American model were within the traditions of the Japanese people. As has been previously reported, they were ready to build further on the tentative experiments in democracy prior to the early 1930s. Their borrowings from the Chinese and Koreans of many centuries before had given them a high regard for education. To make it more available was to join the mainstream of Japanese thinking and priorities. China, and therefore its pupil Japan, had always thought education of first importance, in contrast to many European countries. Japan had greatly improved on its borrowings from China, but American-induced change would be accepted, as had Chinese practice, on Japanese terms. The example of Article 1 of the 1886 Imperial University Order illustrates well the differences in American and Japanese traditional attitudes to education: 'Imperial University has as its goal the teaching of, and the fundamental research into, arts and sciences *necessary for the state*'. Such differences fed American suspicion of Japan's good intentions during the Occupation years, and often produced frustration and apparent deviousness in Japanese officials and educationalists.

Of this period Professor Makoto Yamaguchi writes (*Community Education: A Challenge to Internationalism in Japan*, unpublished paper, 1989): 'The shift in values that took place under the United States occupation, from militarism and ultra-nationalism to democratic ideas, was a Copernican change for the Japanese. Basically, the United States occupation policy aimed to inculcate three principles: internationalism, pacifism and democracy. It was emphasised that Japan should carry out a policy of international co-operation and that an environment should be created that would enable them to discard their insular attitudes and increase their intellectual exchange with foreign countries'. The latter role would be easy to re-establish as it was one of long experience to the Japanese. As R. Rubinger writes of the nineteenth century in his book *Private Academies of Tokugawa Japan* (Princeton University Press, 1982, pp.213–14 and p.223): 'In the final decades of the period, those who combined travel outside their han with political activities and/or training in Dutch, English, other Western languages, Western medicine, sciences of various kinds, and even law, economics, and philosophy began to supplant those in positions of power whose education was limited to

Confucian studies . . . . All this mean that when the country began its modern period, a competent professional class instilled with basic Confucian ideas of service and loyalty but also familiar with the language, technology, and culture of the West, well-travelled and experienced in political, military, and intellectual endeavours, and showing an acceptance of change already existed and had received extensive training'. By 1872 the Meiji Government was employing 214 foreign experts (of whom 119 were British) to supplement the knowledge of the professional class. But it was a process of harnessing foreign know-how to make Japan strong enough to resist those alien things it wished to exclude.

The Japanese, despite the isolation from much of the world during the Tokugawa Shogunate and a certain degree of self-absorbing imperialism from 1931 to 1945, have a strong tradition of looking to other countries for good ideas. This thought is always with me in Japanese hotels where, inevitably, at some point in time the seductive chords of 'Greensleeves' will reach the ear, frequently as if the establishment has only one tape. With good reason the Americans were not as sure of Japanese internationalism. The United States Education Mission to Japan submitted its report to the Supreme Commander for the Allied Powers in Tokyo on 30 March 1946. It recognised in its early pages the power of history and tradition in Japan: 'Our greatest hope . . . is in the children. Sustaining, as they do, the weight of the future, they must not be pressed down by the heritage of a heavy past'. That tradition was seen as having good points which could be built upon: 'For a period of years following the First World War currents of liberal thought were fostered largely by men and women educated in the colleges and universities of Japan. Higher education now has the opportunity of again setting a standard of free thought, bold enquiry, and hopeful action for the people. To fulfil these purposes, higher education should become an opportunity for the many, not a privilege of the few'. In fact only America is surpassing Japan in the percentage of the population attending higher education, but its achievement is based on the enthusiasm and self-sacrifice of the private individual, not notably the support of the state. Similarly, the intellectual debate about Japanese society may be lively in many universities, but higher education is largely ignored by government and business. Businessmen tolerate the universities as a selection process which makes executive recruitment easy for them. They know the best students go to the Universities of Tokyo and Kyoto. They wish to train them when they graduate from their four years of, for the company, largely irrelevant study as they see it. With the British ruthlessly élitist higher education system in mind I have found the Japanese attempt to achieve what the American proposed very attractive, but again Professor Uesugi warned of the dangers: 'In some private universities the staff/student ratio is very poor. Industry often does not believe in higher education, but thinks the bright people go there and must be recruited. Younger men in particular do not want to gain the skills of a craftsman, but prefer to go to college. Those who cannot go to the prestige universities may go to a much inferior private university. Low academic ability people may be sent to very poor private universities to avoid the stigma of poor performance. Well over 90 per cent of the age group go to senior high school. Taxi drivers may be private university graduates'. As the Americans wished, Japan has a mass higher education system, but there may be times when the Japanese are not sure that the United States Education Mission was being ironic or not when writing, 'The University is the crown of every modern educational system'. A mass higher education system, unless given an absolute national priority in the allocation of resources, seems doomed to have its Harvards at one end and its University of Cow Patch at the other end of the scale of material well-being and quality of provision. As will be further noted later, the Japanese government has been frugal in funding higher education, so that most of its finance comes from parents and the private sector (churches rather than business).

The Mission noted that 'During this period of crisis for the Japanese people, Adult Education is of paramount importance, for a democratic state places much responsibility on each citi-zen . . . . evening and extension classes for adults, and the opening of buildings to a variety of community activities . . . library service in all prefectures . . . organizations of all kinds, including community and professional societies, labor unions, and political groups, should be helped to use effectively the techniques of forum and discussion'. Again, this proposal fell on fertile ground with the Ministry of Education issuing a circular in July 1946 suggesting that kominkans (that is, community centres and halls) should be established in every town and village. Again, this met well the priorities of the Japanese for reconstructing family and community life after the devastation of the war.

The United States Mission looked to decentralisation as an impor-tant development: 'A highly centralized educational system, even if it is not caught in the net of ultra-nationalism and militarism, is endangered by the evils that accompany an intrenched bureaucracy. Decentralization is necessary in order that teachers may be freed to develop professionally under guidance, without regimentation'. A country which had painfully achieved reunification in the late sixteenth century, then developed a remarkably efficient feudal system with a high degree of centralisation which it passed onto the Meiji government in 1868, was unlikely to risk such achievement because Americans thought local democracy important. Japan remains a highly centralised administration.

In the light of Japanese disarray MacArthur in February 1946 set up his own team to draft a new constitution. On 3 May 1947, with some cosmetic changes by the Japanese, the results were adopted by the government as an amendment to the 1889 Constitution. It is a very American document, but has been generally accepted by the Japanese, beginning, 'We, the Japanese people, acting through our duly elected representatives in the National Diet, determined that we shall secure for ourselves and our posterity the fruits of peaceful cooperation with all nations and the blessings of liberty throughout this land, and resolved that never again shall we be visited with the horrors of war through the action of government, do proclaim that sovereign power resides with the people and do firmly establish this Constitution. Government is a sacred trust of the people, the authority for which is derived from the people, the powers of which are exercised by the representatives of the people, and the benefits of which are enjoyed by the people. This is a universal principle of mankind upon which this Constitution is founded. We reject and revoke all constitutions, laws, ordinances, and rescripts in conflict herewith'.

In March of 1947 the Fundamental Law of Education (Law 25) and the School Education Law were made public. These were followed by the Board of Education Law in 1948, the Social Education Law in 1949, the Public Library Law in 1950, the Museum Law in 1951, and the Youth Classes Promotion Law in 1953. As always, the Japanese were taking educational activities very seriously.

The Fundamental Law of Education set the scene for postwar educational, social and economic revival. To a modern Western audience it is an attractive document, but, as was inevitable, Japanese interpretation has given some points in it greater emphasis than others. Its introduction states, 'Having established the Constitution of Japan, we have shown our resolution to contribute to the peace of the world and welfare of humanity by building a democratic and cultural state.

The realization of this ideal shall depend fundamentally on the power of education. We shall esteem individual dignity and endeavour to bring up the people who love truth and peace, while education which aims at the creation of culture general and rich individuality shall be spread far and wide. We hereby enact this Law in accordance with the spirit of the Constitution of Japan, with a view to clarifying the aim of education and establishing the foundation of education for new Japan'. The Americans were determined to bring in their tradition of education, being for the benefit of the individual, not primarily for the state. Again, this was obviously against Japanese traditions and was to be quickly modified in practice.

Article 1 of the Law was entitled 'Aim of Education' and continued the theme of individuality: 'Education shall aim at the full development of personality, striving for the rearing of the people, sound in mind and body, who shall love truth and justice, esteem individual value, respect labour and have a deep sense of responsibility, and be imbued with the independent spirit, as builders of the peaceful state and society'. As the vast majority of Japanese wished to be part of a group and to progress by consensus, American style independent spirit was to prove elusive. Article 2 was on 'Educational Principle': 'The aim of education shall be realized on all occasions and in all places. In order to achieve the aim, we shall endeavour to contribute to the creation and development of culture by mutual esteem and cooperation, respecting academic freedom, having a regard for actual life and cultivating a spontaneous spirit'. As the whole Japanese culture was based on cooperation that part of Article 2 was easy to accommodate, but more difficulty would come from interesting Japanese in exercising a spontaneous spirit. Article 3 was entitled 'Equal Opportunity in Education': 'The people shall all be given equal opportunities of receiving education according to their ability, and shall not be subject to educational discrimination on account of race, creed, sex, social status, economic position, or family origin. The state and local public bodies shall take measures to give financial assistance to those who have, with all their ability, difficulty in receiving education for economic reasons'. Great progress has been made on these issues since 1947. The educational inequalities in Japan are much less than those in Britain. However, women are at some disadvantage after 18 in the higher education system, as in the better job rat race. As a racist society such minorities as the Koreans are often less well served, whilst the Burakumin (Special Village People) have experienced severe discrimination. The two to three million Burakumin are thought to be Japanese descended from their low status of the Edo Era, 'many of these factors are derivatives from occupation. The concept of pollution, for example, is an appropriate case illlustrating an association between Burakumin occupations and the belief in contamination' (N. Shimahara, p.18). However, it would seem likely that the lower status accorded them by the Shogunate restricted what their occupation could be, which then reinforced their low status. Whatever the origin of Japan's Special Village People, they are still discriminated against and their numbers in higher education are very low. Article 4 was entitled 'Compulsory Education': 'The people shall be obligated to have boys and girls under their protection receive nine years general education. No tuition fee shall be charged for compulsory education in schools established by the state and local bodies'. The 1941 Regulation on Elementary Education had proposed compulsory education from six years to 14, but had not been implemented so that in 1945 some children had only six years of schooling. Only one in five elementary pupils went on to the secondary schools and the remainder went to upper elementary schools and youth schools, and there was only 3.7 per cent of teenage cohort at university in 1940. Article 4 would be popular with the Japanese, although resourcing it initially proved difficult. Article 5 on 'Co-education' demonstrated the American determination to use education to improve the status of women: 'Men and women shall esteem and cooperate with each other. Co-education, therefore, shall be recognized in education'. And co-education has remained the norm in most of Japan's education system, with notable exceptions again found in higher education. The Fundamental Law of Education then continued with a further six Articles in much the same style.

   Co-education has had some impact on equality for women. Whenever Kenji Miwa introduces a female friend or colleague to me he will say that Japanese women are repressed, 'But she is an exception'. I seem to meet women who are always 'the exception to the rule of the down-trodden Japanese female'. Some of these are predictable. On my visits to the National Women's Education Centre, a matter of some pleasure, those who run it are as self-confident as any European woman. I am looked after by the capable Ms Hiroko Hashimoto, who is the Head of the Information and International Exchange Division, but she is partly American educated (Berkeley), whilst the elegant Director General, Mizue Maeda, spent many years in France and Britain, and has the familiar charisma of a senior civil servant. Powerful

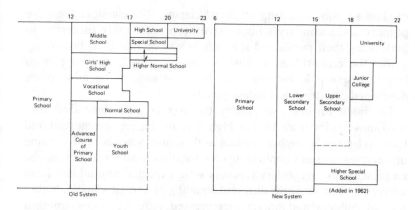

SOURCE From Kojiro Kishimoto and Shigekazu Takemura, 'Education in Japan after 1945'; *Education in Japan*, vol. I, 1966.

FIGURE 5.1 *A Comparison of New and Old School Systems*

personalities like Professor Kazuyo Yamamoto can combine authoritative national and international roles with more traditional Japanese skills. When my new British jacket started shedding buttons in a Tokyo hotel Professor Yamamoto combined both Japanese charm and housewifely skill in sewing them back on. And yet when we left the hotel there was no doubt who was in charge. For less exceptional women inequality remains.

The School Education Law introduced in detail the new so-called 6–3–3–4 system, that is six years of primary school, three years of lower secondary school, three years of upper secondary school, and four years of university. This was to replace the 6–5–3–3 model (six years of primary school, five years of middle school, three years of high school, and three years of university). The changes are usefully illustrated in Figure 5.1. As will be clear, compulsory education was to cover the six years of primary education and three years of lower secondary schooling. The upper secondary school was to be open to as many children as wanted to attend; as has been mentioned, such attendance is now almost universal. In 1953 it was 36 per cent. The changes were meant to encourage greater access to later schooling by a single-track system. In this the Act has been more successful than the most optimistic American in 1947 would have forecast. But it is worth pointing out that from the first modern educational developments in the late nineteenth century there was a tradition of state schools attracting all social classes. The classless Japanese primary and secondary schools have been remarkably successful in persuading their pupils and students to stay on into their late teens, unlike the crisis-ridden English secondary school, and have been largely responsible for creating, by the standards of most other developed countries, a classless society.

To widen further opportunity the Act created some five hundred universities from former high schools, higher commercial and technical schools, higher normal and normal schools, and existing universities. Besides confirming co-education in all levels of schools, all primary and secondary teachers were expected to graduate from university. The previous different standing of normal schools, higher normal colleges and universities created differing status amongst teachers.

The Board of Education Law of 1948 was an effort to do something about the United States Mission's strong criticism of the high centralisation of Japan's educational administration. Each locality was to have a board of education which was to be independent of other local bodies. The 1949 Ministry of Education Organisation Law aimed at curbing directly Tokyo's power. The Minister of Education was not to exercise 'any administrative or executive direction or supervision'; the Department of Education was to become a servicing, advisory and technical ministry. Teachers were to be given much greater autonomy. As the ever careful Reischauer wrote (p.194), 'The control of public education has been a matter of hot political contention ever since the war. Mindful of the role of the prewar educational system in militaristic indoctrination, the American occupation insisted on the dispersal of educational controls to elected prefectural and municipal boards of education, somewhat in the American manner, but subsequently the Japanese in part recentralized the system under the Ministry of Education. Prefectural and municipal education boards remain, but they are appointed by governors and mayors, not elected, and, though they have the right to select the text-books and these are produced privately, all textbooks must first receive ministry approval'. As always, it is dangerous to move too fast from the historic cultural traditions. In the end less change results. Japan's education system remains under central government control, as was the intention of the samurai and merchants who usurped power in the 1860s.

Article 7 of the Fundamental Law of Education was aimed at encouraging social education with national and local public bodies exhorted to provide libraries, museums, kominkans (community centres), make greater community use of school facilities, and generally encourage educational pursuits at work, in the home, and elsewhere. Similarly, Article 10 directed the education authorities to make provision of facilities to encourage the citizens' education. With this as a background the 1949 Social Education Law defined the roles of national and local education bodies. For example, the boards of education of cities, town and villages were to establish community centres and halls, provide youth classes, establish libraries, museums and other facilities, offer and/or encourage other agencies to offer courses, publish and distribute information on technical and vocational education, and arrange and provide facilities for social education. The prefectural boards of education were to co-ordinate and encourage the activities of the local boards, offer training for their staffs, and provide the sort of larger-scale facilities in social education beyond the scope of the local boards. Central government would subsidise local boards, establish national facilities for social education, and develop useful materials for the field. Initially Article 13 of the Act prohibited the granting of financial subsidies to voluntary organisations, which has been one of the great strengths of the British system, but the weakness of the voluntary sector saw this amended in 1959.

To reflect public interest social education committees were established composed of representatives of voluntary bodies, school principals and other worthy citizens. The kominkans had similar advisory committees. Article 20 stated that the kominkans should offer educational and cultural programmes related to the life of the people to promote their health, culture and welfare. Article 22 added that the kominkans should provide debates, lectures, exhibitions, and recreational activities, and also youth classes. The kominkans were to be available to the people of the local community, but not for political parties' activities or religious organisations or those wishing to make a financial profit. They were to fit in with the aim of Social Education of providing 'systematic educational activities for youth and adults (including physical exercise and recreation) excluding educational activities as in the school curriculum'. As might be expected in a Japan still trying to recover from its devastation in the war, by 1951 a majority of the 6793 main halls and 16 391 branch halls which had been set up had no building. This is in contrast to the modern kominkan which frequently occupies a magnificent building and site.

The 1950 Public Library Act, as also the Museum Act of the following year, was an attempt to change libraries for an under-utilised resource favoured by a small minority of the citizens. Libraries were to offer their services to all citizens, and to extend such facilities from not only book lending, but to reference services, courses, lectures, films, and other roles familiar to the West. Similarly, museums were to be places of cultural activity, not only places to preserve the past. Both libraries and museums were moved centre-stage in the field of social education, and their staffs were expected to act professionally and thus be qualified accordingly.

The 1953 Youth Classes Promotion Act was part of the group of laws, although it comes outside the period of the American Occupation. It permitted financial aid to be given to local authorities which open classes related to the voluntary youth movement which had been a notable part of rural Japan since 1945. Youth schools had first been set up in 1930 (youth training centres had been established in 1926), and made compulsory in 1939. They had been closed when the Americans arrived, which cut off those over 15 from an opportunity to improve their formal education. In response, study circles of a voluntary nature on various subjects were established in the countryside. The law encouraged such classes in all parts of Japan, from cities to villages, and the national government was to provide financial aid to local government for the purpose. To qualify for such aid the class had to have more than 30 members, and pursue over a hundred hours of study in a year. The teaching staff had to be qualified. From 13 628 youth classes with 892 087 students in 1952 such provision increased to 17 606 classes with 1 091 734 students in 1955.

There was a steady growth in adult education classes during the Occupation, greatly encouraged by both central and local government. By the early 1950s some 20 000 such classes were being provided by local public bodies. Whilst the 1946 United States Mission had warmly recommended the establishing of parent-teacher associations, Americans were hostile to 'women's classes' as this was thought to undermine equal rights for men and women. It was only after the end of the Occupation that such provision again became apparent. The PTAs initially built on the prewar tradition of being fund raisers for hard pressed schools, but the 1960 Local Government Financial Act forbade the collecting of money for provision which should be funded from local taxes so parents' organisations could no longer provide money for schools. The PTAs then began expanding their cultural activities and promoting courses and lectures aimed at helping parents' understanding of education. Of the PTAs Merry White writes of their role in the later 1980s (p.63):

As in the educational changes of the nineteenth century, reform of the content of the postwar curriculum posed little problem; it was the restructuring of educational *institutions* which strained society's adaptive powers. While abstract concepts such as 'democratic values' were well received after the war, the concrete decentralization of school bureaucracies, among other changes, met resistance. However, with a few substantive changes, at least initially, the American model was adopted, and local school boards, the P-TA, and the Teachers' Union became fixtures in the environment of the school. In fact, the latter two organizations have become more powerful and active in their transplanted form than in the American originals: the P-TA as a kind of ritualized therapy 'club' for anxious mothers, as well as a training ground for women learning to take roles in public activities; and the Teachers' Union as the largest union in Japan, characterized by its strong leftist opposition to the ministry of education and to the mainstream establishment at large.

The cultural attitudes towards and among Japanese women in 1945 highlight the difficulties faced by an American administration determined to produce major social change in the country. Japanese society had a very clear view of women's role. America might enfranchise women in Japan, but it would take more than legislation to change several centuries of tradition. Whilst education would be the great modifier of female inequality, by Western standards women still seem at a disadvantage to men in Japan.

The distance to be travelled in order to achieve equality of the sexes beginning in 1945 is usefully illustrated by a book produced in 1937 by the teaching staff of the Tokyo Higher Normal School for Women, and published by Kenkyusha. The contributors were amongst the best educated and 'enlightened' women of Japan prior to the Second World War. The view from the rural areas might have been expected to be more oppressive. The book was entitled *Life of the Japanese Woman of To-day*. It was aimed at an international audience, funding coming from Kokusai Bunka Shinkokai (the Society for International Cultural Relations).

In the Preface President Juichi Shimomura of the Tokyo Normal School for Women described the volume as a collection of pictures and continued, 'Home life occupies, and has occupied throughout the ages, the most important sphere of the life of the Japanese woman. It will do so tomorrow, and for all the days to come. The problem confronting her at the present moment, is not a question of neglecting the home, but how she can combine her social activities with the proper discharge of her own home duties. How can she be trained to meet these two demands is a matter of grave concern to us, the educationists'.

It is a short book of four chapters entitled 'Women and Home Life in Japan', 'Domestic Education in Japan', 'Vocational Life of Women in Japan', and 'Social Activities of Women in Japan'. It might have been a reminder to the Americans in 1945 that even in the great city of Tokyo, for all its interest in the West from the nineteenth century onwards, Japanese social assumptions were not the same as those of Europe or North America. It was a foreign country with a long and distinguished history.

The first chapter was subdivided into four. 'Japanese Love of Home' was followed by 'Home Life of Japan To-day', 'Diversity of Japanese Home Life of To-day', and, perhaps significantly, 'Still Quite Japanese'. The chapter opened with the statement, 'Country and Home are the two objects nearest to the heart of the Japanese people. This is a truth established through long history, and will forever remain unchanged. Although this sentiment may not be confined solely to Japanese – indeed, the same can be said of the people of other countries – yet this is a special Japanese characteristic, for our people have unified love of country with love of home'. Some of the writing now seems very dated, but the sentiments expressed are clear: 'It is our belief that loyalty to the Emperor is identical with filial piety, and without loyalty there is no filial piety, and without filial piety there is no loyalty'; 'When their sons are about to go to war, it is no unusual thing in Japan for parents to encourage them with the words, "Fight bravely for the country, my son, and that will bring great honour to our family". And the son replies, "Please do not worry, my parents, for I will do my best for our country, and never will I stain the honour of the family". This is the heart-felt cry of a Japanese, in whom loyalty and filial piety are united'; 'what counts most is its shrine, and it is this which connotes the Japanese home'. As in the study of any foreign culture, a major problem is the different meaning the same word can have in two societies. In Britain the word 'home' conjures up a range of meanings and emotions; for the Japanese of the later 1930s there were often dissimilar emphases: 'the Japanese love of home is expressed in the spirit of service and sacrifice. This spirit is the essence of the family life of Japan'. A familiar criticism is of 'selfish individualism' as against the much praised 'spirit of sacrifice'. Of Japanese women the writer contended, 'The Japanese wife's devotion to her husband, her dutifulness to her husband's family, her obedience to her husband's parents, her diligence to her daily tasks; these and many other virtues are due, not to any weakness or docility in the Japanese woman, but to her noble spirit of self-sacrifice'. Whilst there were what were called 'New Women' in Japan in the 1930s who were dissatisfied with the allocated role of good wives and wise mothers (ryosai kembo), alternatives to a traditional marital life were few and 'the chastity, obedience, diligence of Japanese women are not the results of their docility, but are the fruits of their training' the writer informed the readers.

The changes which followed Japan's industrialisation, such as the move to the cities with resulting smaller families, had already produced a modified attitude to housewives who had previously been noted for their invisibility (Kanai, or someone who confines herself to the house). The urban home was a place of consumption, whilst the farm was a centre of production. In the light of this women, as the organisers of the urban house, were given a much more dominant role. However, it is worth stating again that full urbanisation in Japan did not take place until the 1950s and 1960s and may help to explain some of the reasons why, as Professor Makoto Yamaguchi points out ('Feminism and Adult Education in Japan', unpublished, June 1988), 'The modern Japanese women's movement started in August 1971, when the first nation-wide meeting of women's liberationists was held in Nagoya with twelve hundred participants. They were from non-political and grass-roots groups'. This is notably later than in countries of North America and Western Europe. Rural societies are always conservative and traditional. Nevertheless, social change was acknowledged, even in 1937 under a government stressing traditional roles.

Under 'Still Quite Japanese' the author explored 'the rising tide in Japan which tends to re-examine the value of our own culture in contrast to foreign culture' amidst a feeling that Japan should not repeat 'the unwisdom of attempting to imitate indiscriminately foreign culture and manners as they did some 50 years ago'.

When Merry White writes (p.13) in 1987, 'Mothers are intensely committed to their children from the onset of pregnancy and see their major life's task as the rearing of successful children', she is confirming the survival of Japan's often unchanging culture. In 1937 the 'Mission fo Japanese Women' referred to 'the retention fo the innate Japanese spirit, in spite of the influx of foreign modes of living . . . Though they wear foreign clothes, live in foreign houses, consume foreign food, play foreign music and master foreign etiquette, yet they maintain intact the spirit of Japanese womanhood . . . Contact with a different set of virtues from abroad only causes them to shine with greater radiance. In the next place we must draw attention to the fact that Japanese women are making great efforts towards the realization of good motherhood. They are earnestly trying to develop their mothers' tender instinct on a scientific basis, and to promote the understanding of child education. In these matters they are trained at school, but they never cease to continue to educate themselves, even after becoming mothers. Such is the conspicuous tendency seen in recent years. Nor do they confine their interest in motherhood to their own homes, but extend it to broader fields in social activities. Activities, such as the Parent-Teachers Association, and social work . . . . are examples of this maternal spirit. It is true that in Japan we have witnessed the evolution fo the vocational woman, and her intense social activities. Yet in the final analysis, home life is the object of her interest and ideals . . . . Japanese women distinguish themselves as good wives and good home-makers. And does not the fame of good home-maker bring honour to a woman'. Of course, it is important to recall that most British wives were 'home-makers' in 1937. The Second World War brought further developments in social change, with the United Kingdom now having perhaps the highest percentage of women in full-time employment. Even in the Japan of the mid-1980s of women over 15 years of age 49 per cent were in employment, whilst 31.6 per cent kept house. Women made up 35.6 per cent of those employed in Japan in 1984. In 1960 women employed outside the home numbered 7.38 million, which more than doubled to 15.18 million in 1984. In 1984 29.2 per cent of all married women were in employment. This is very low by British standards, but does represent substantial change in Japan's traditions.

Prewar Japanese schools were tooled-up to confirm the allotted role in society for women. Domestic science began in the primary school and girls continued with such studies throughout the high schools. Girls were introduced to classes in sewing in the fourth grade, 'fostering the habit of utilization and conservation of materials'; in the higher primary school Home Management was taught, 'The government regulations require the teaching of a general knowledge of food, clothing, and habitation, besides nursing, bringing-up children and household economics'. In the high schools for girls home management was part of the last two years of the course and included Arrangement of the home, Sanitation in the home, Preparation of food, Child rearing, Care and nursing of the aged, Household economy, and Domestic budget (Department of Education instructions). Such studies continued in the Normal and Higher Normal Schools.

Chapter Three on the 'Vocational Life of Women in Japan' was again divided into three sections, 'Diligence of Japanese Women', 'Various Aspects of Women's Vocations', 'Vocational Women and Marriage'. It opens with, 'Diligence is the characteristic trait of Japanese women. They serve in their homes as wives, mothers, and housekeepers, taking all responsibility for the management of the home. The quiet modesty and joy which she brings to her work are counted as the virtues of a Japanese woman'.

In women in work in 1937 601 out of every 1000 were engaged in farming, as against, say, 55 in textile work, or 15 in the manufacture of clothing and accessories, or 12 in education. The domination of agricultural employment prewar was obvious, but this also meant that out of every 1000 female workers 581 were married. Japan's economy of 1937 was very different from that of the late twentieth century, with the family farm a much more central factor. In farming 714 female workers out of every 1000 were married. As the writer stated, without any sense of irony, 'one of the chief qualifications for a bride is that she must possess good health and ability to work. This is especially true in the rural life of today'. In contrast in industry 396 women in every 1000 female workers were married, or 26 out of every 1000 domestic servants.

The final chapter on 'Social Activities of Women in Japan' confirmed the obvious fact that a society's attitudes are shaped by its history. As in Britain the Japanese are constantly aware of their history. The author pointed out that, 'During feudal times, the dearly-loved daughter of the family was called 'hakoiri-musume', the literal translation of which is 'daughter kept in a box', and she was actually shut up in the house and cherished like a doll'. The role of women before 1868 was as private individuals, 'service and self-sacrifice were required of them as members of the family and not of society'. Of course, life in Western Europe at this time was very much male oriented, but perhaps we are discussing matters of degree.

After the Meiji Restoration a weak women's movement began, but the drift of females into the new industries began to change the aspirations of some women. In 1919 Akiko Kyokwai led The New Women's Federation with a programme demanding equal opportunities for women and 'full development of women's capacities', co-operation between men and women to achieve this, to 'elucidate the social significance of the home', and the protection of the rights of women, mothers, and children. The 1923 earthquake resulted in considerable cooperation between women's groups for the first time. Afterwards 47 women's societies came together to form the Tokyo Federated Women's Association in support of women's movements, social work, reforms in public morals, research, lectures, and training courses. The passing of the Universal Manhood Suffrage Bill in 1924 saw the Association as a major promoter of the Women's League for the Acquisition of the Franchise, the latter declaring, 'The women of our country, regardless of their differences in sentiment, religion, or ideas, should combine in the name of womanhood, and concentrate their efforts to obtain women's suffrage as their sole aim. Of course, the acquisition of women's suffrage does not mean the solution of all our problems, nor does it mean the birth of an ideal society. But women's suffrage, as such, is the most expedient and effective solution to such problems as women's education problems, women's legal status problems, women's labour problems, and moral problems, etc., and is the one sure way of promoting the welfare of our society and state'.

In 1931 the government introduced a Bill for Women's Franchise into the Fifty-Ninth Session of the Diet. The House of Representatives passed the Bill, but it was defeated in the House of Peers. The writer notes afterwards, 'With the outbreak of the Manchurian Incident in 1931, the women's patriotic movement suddenly became active and the movement was carried on systematically throughout Japan and included all of the existing as well as new organizations. This is one of the most important movements which has been going on among Japanese women in recent years'. The second section of the chapter was on 'Social Work Carried on by Japanese Women'. After an explanation of the role of the Imperial Family, and some history, there was a listing of the more

important organisations such as the Women's Patriotic Front with
2 200 000 members, and the Women's National Defence Association
with 1 920 000 members ('Our organization comprises as its basis, the
spirit of the nation-wide conscription system and has for its purpose
the manifestation of the true Japanese womanhood, fulfillment of the
great duty of national defence and support of the soldiers from behind
the lines'). Amongst the latter's purposes was 'To train children of
our country thoroughly both in spirit and body, so that they can fulfil
their duty for the defence of the country'.

A section on 'Political Activities of Japanese Women' gave a brief
history up to 1937, and dealt mainly with the abortive efforts to
gain women's suffrage. Section IV was on the 'Movement for the
Promotion of Learning Among Japanese Women', and reported
that appeals to the government 'for the extension and enlargement
of women's educational facilities...have met with no favourable
response'. Section V, 'Labour Movement of Japanese Women',
reported poor working conditions, but concluded, 'In short, the
solution of these problems must be left to the future. The women's
activities in the line of protection and improvement of the condition
of working women are at present as inactive as the aforesaid
movement for the promotion of learning among women, and are
hardly worthy of any special comment here'.

The book's concluding paragraphs are a useful summary of the
position of Japanese women just eight years before the Americans
arrived to try to turn their world upside down:

> This much, then, may be said of the activities of Japanese women
> in politics, education, social work, and labour movement. We
> have seen that their most important activities are in social work and
> military relief work, which include social education, protection
> and relief, and goodwill. Next come the activities in women's
> suffrage and the promotion of learning among women, while
> the women's labour movement remains the most inactive among
> them all. But what we have to notice is that in none of these
> movements is shown such a radical attitude in Japanese women
> as to thoroughly ignore or entirely cut off the connection with the
> family system, of which they are members. Though there are some
> exceptions, Japanese women as a whole are of such a gentle nature
> as to be unable to identify themselves exclusively with public-
> spirited women or to demand complete freedom for their lives.
> It is impossible for them to cut off their connection with the home

life, and we may take it for granted that such an indefinite attitude would not cause much satisfaction to some radical reformers. Shall we not say, then, that it is the characteristic trait of Japanese women that even while they are busily engaging in social activities, their minds will never wander far from their homes?

In 1984 women voters made up 51.6 per cent of the electorate, but only 1.6 per cent of the members of the House of Representatives and 7.7 per cent of the (upper) House of Councillors in 1986. Whilst almost all girls now go on to upper secondary school, and 34.5 per cent of the female age cohort enter institutions of higher education, it is to the two-year junior colleges that over 60 per cent of them flock, as Professor Uesugi stated, whilst 95.2 per cent of the boys going on to higher education enter four or more years of university programme. The modern figures emphasise how relatively recent in a country's history 1937, or even 1868, is. As the National Women's Education Centre bus leaves its beautiful grounds the (male) guards on the gate stand to attention and salute. It is smart gesture, flattering to the occupants, and suggesting another example of Japanese efficiency. And yet . . .

More than anything else women are the indicators of social change in Japan. The Americans were quick to realise this when they came in September 1945, but mainly failed in their abrupt efforts to launch a revolution. There *has* been great change in the position of women in Japan since 1945, and that is speeding up. In the main, however, the education system has been a force for conservatism rather than a support of such change.

The seventh-grade girls' elementary school textbooks the Americans inherited when they arrived included the words, 'The entire nation must cooperate for the war effort, and at the same time, we girls should exert our abilities to the maximum. War and the position of women are closely connected. Women whose fathers, sons, and husbands went out to war, should produce the bullets and weapons used by them. On the other hand, women should also prepare food and clothing, and keep their homes, native places and their country from the invasion by enemy planes . . . It must be kept in mind that the duty of the woman of our Empire begins with the valuable life of mother. For that purpose, you should cultivate yourselves. Especially, under the present situation, it is important that you cultivate self-confidence and develop your potential to meet any difficulties as a substitute for men being in the battle field'. Wars usually promote selective social change, but this has to contend with a desire amongst the war weary to return to familiar ways.

A good assessment of the problems which beset Japanese education in late 1945 is made by Professors Toshihiko Saito and Eiichi Ameda in *The Modernization of Japanese Education* (International Society for Educational Information, Tokyo, 1986, volume 1, pp.37-8):

The first was the promotion of standardization. As previously mentioned, Japan's modernization was due to strong government leadership and national guidance. This same characteristic of national guidance became manifest in the important role played by education in the promotion of modernization. Here, excessive state control was brought to bear on education, from its administration through to the curriculum, accelerating the standardization of education. Standardization was thought ideal to mould the national consciousness. For example, the preparation of textbooks was nationalized. Total loyalty to the state was emphasized, particularly in the ethics and morality course. Second, problems arose from the formation of concepts of individuality and individual rights. If a national consciousness was to be created, an individual's sense of his or her own rights and a consciousness of human rights could only be encouraged half-heartedly. Instead of a modern consciousness of human rights, nationalistic patriotism was inculcated, concentrating on the importance of the state. Thus, the result of the policy of strengthening defence and national prosperity was the birth of militarism. The third problem was the borrowed nature of the knowledge being taught. In promoting the government's policies of modernization and industrialization, the policy adopted for the introduction of science and technology was to borrow the knowledge wholesale from the West. The means of propagation of this knowledge did not support its germination into real learning or scientific thinking. An education centred on rote memory and written tests came into existence mainly because the rapid spread of knowledge became an end in itself. This closed the door to the evolution and modernization of Japan's highly developed and cultivated tradition and enervated its indigenous creative potential. The fourth problem was the importance attached to written tests. The placing weight on a person's school record, which had been brought about by closely linking the school system and the mechanism for selecting and developing talented people, greatly intensified entrance exam competition because students were ambitious to obtain higher social positions and higher posts. Education became a matter of just passing examinations. Furthermore, since the selection of capable people occurred mainly in the schools, a school-centred view of education was created. The fifth problem is called the double structure of education. Efficient training courses for an élite of talented people were differentiated from other courses and, in terms of educational history, a nineteenth-century type of school system called the 'double-track' system was created. This brought about inequalities in educational opportunity at secondary and higher levels of education.

Two major factors might have been expected to aid the Americans in, as we have seen, their determination to tackle these problems. After the educational stagnation of the 1930s and 1940s, plus military defeat and occupation by a foreign power for the first time in Japanese history, perhaps a majority of the Japanese were willing to see some form of educational change. Secondly, the education system had been largely destroyed. Rebuilding in new ways might be possible. But it is worth stressing once more that people are slow to change. To achieve this there is a need to recognise strong traditions and the always powerful factor of history. Beginning with Article 26 of the Constitution, which gave the Japanese the right to receive education, the Occupation forces built with enthusiasm. Much success resulted, for example, in promoting equal educational opportunity which saw over 90 per cent of the age cohort going onto senior high school by 1974 and, by 1976, those attending institutions of higher education reaching 39 per cent. Britain would envy such figures.

Similarly, as already noted, a single-track school system was successfully implemented, compulsory education extended to nine years, civil rights confirmed, and attempts made to enhance individuality amongst pupils and students, and to decentralise educational administration. It was no surprise that a largely American Occupation force should endeavour to introduce mainly American models. This was not unreasonable as American education looked good in 1945. And Japan still has much to learn from it, particularly at the higher education level. However, other people's institutional models and associated assumptions have to be introduced with sensitivity. As has been emphasised there was, and is, no part of Japanese life which was, or is, more greatly prized and regarded than Education. As the President of Hiroshima University proclaimed in 1970 (*Education in Japan*, volume V, 1970), 'Japan has grown into one of the modern nations, ranking favourably with Western countries in the course of only one century since the beginning of the Meiji Era. We must not forget the fact that the foundation for this development was laid essentially by the power of education, and to a lesser extent by political and economic power'. Japanese high regard for education has much to teach a Britain anxious to regain its economic momentum.

As Professor Hajime Tajima confirms in *The Modernization of Japanese Education* (pp.23–4):

It is, however, apparent that the consciousness and lifestyle of the prewar society had not been mature enough to unconditionally welcome or support the rapid and independent reform of the educational system that occurred after the war . . . . The fact that the guiding hand of postwar reforms belonged to the U.S. Occupation authorities, and not to the independent will of the Japanese people, later gave the Japanese government an excuse to change the direction of the reforms and regain control over national education. One representative example of this is the change of the selection method for the education board in 1956 from public election to official appointment. Also, a fixed 'course of study' or curriculum was introduced, and screening of school textbooks by the Ministry of Education became much stricter. Thus, the government regained control over the content of national education . . . . Industrial circles expected education to develop human resources that would support the growth of the economy and tried to see their demands reflected in state policies. The Ministry of Education at last bowed to intensified pressure from this sector and altered the direction of postwar educational reforms. Using the motto 'development of science and technology', the ministry completely revised its 'course of study' in 1958 toward a standardized curriculum and reinforced its control over education. It also carried out nationwide academic ability tests and (as previously mentioned) changed the method of selection of the board of education. Thus, administrative guidance for the education system by the government became stricter.

The tradition of centralisation and looking to authority, whether group derived consensus or governmental, dies hard. Those who stay at Japanese hotels will often be surprised by the number of instructions the resident faces to ensure conformity. 'Please feel free to wear the Yukata kimono on your bed. Please wear the Yukata only in your room'; would I dare get off the bed in it? At the same hotel which favoured such wording I ordered a Japanese breakfast at a bar arrangement. In halting English the young man next to me was a pillar of patience in explaining how I should tackle the meal. I had not solicited his help, but it was spontaneously and generously provided as an extra duty in a busy Tokyo day. Unlike most Japanese he did not give me his name card, but I found out that he was an engineer who helped design hi-fi equipment. The cultural traditions of Japan have much to recommend them. Besides the great courtesy shown by the vast majority of people, there are other practical advantages such as a very low crime rate. It is possible to wander around any large city in Japan in safety at any hour. This simple pleasure is more difficult to gain in West European towns. When meeting again Professor Motoaki Hagiwara of Gumma University in 1989 I asked how his trip to Europe that year had gone, and received the simple reply, 'Mugged and robbed in Paris'.

But such strong traditions can work against desirable innovation and change, and the reaction to much of the educational reform of the period of the American Occupation demonstrated this. Education in Japan has a very long history, as the writings of such distinguished scholars as R.P. Dore have brought home to the West. As he stated in a paper in 1965 ('the Legacy of Tokugawa Education', in M.B. Jansen (editor), *Changing Attitudes Toward Modernization*, Princeton UP), 'Those who look hopefully to Japan for "lessons" in how late-comers can industrialize and build effective national political institutions are apt to overlook one important respect in which mid-nineteenth century Japan differed from its Asian neighbours and from most of those societies which still count as underdeveloped today – Japan already had a developed system of formal school education. It was a system which was largely swept away in the modernizing enthusiasm of the 1870s, and it was a system which in many respects had to be swept away if Japan was to emerge as a modern industrial and military power. It was class-ridden, formalistic, backward-looking, out-of-date. But it was also intellectually sophisticated, disciplined, occasionally stimulating, and politically relevant. Whatever one's judgement of its value, the fact remains that this system shaped the generation which, in the last quarter of the nineteenth century, carried through the sweeping changes which laid the foundation of modern Japan'. In *Private Academies of Tokugawa Japan* R. Rubinger (pp.211–12 and p.223) gives a description of the educational system of pre-Restoration Japan which inculcated many of the attitudes still found in its culture:

The fundamental first stage of all those who rose to positions of leadership, whether samurai or commoner was Chinese studies. This was not only the road to basic literacy, but was the prerequisite to advanced study of all kinds . . . Chinese studies for samurai and commoners typically began at home with a tutor – parents, relatives, or a paid professional. This continued until the age of eight or ten when a child went off to school, and might well continue after that if the family could afford it. Beyond the basic level of home tutorial the possibilities for schooling were varied. Commoners could attend a local terakoya, a low-level shijuku, or go into apprenticeship training. For the samurai class, there was diversity even at the early stages of schooling due to the differences in availability, quality, and levels of han school offerings. Some han schools provided only the basic rudiments of learning; others only advanced studies . . . . In the relatively more stable Japan of the late seventeenth and eighteenth centuries the official schools had functioned well in educating the leadership class in the values of the state, the emphasis on ritual and observance of distinctions of age, sex, social class and rank were instilled along with respect for authority within a frame of reference defined by feudal obligations. Sons followed in hereditary succession the occupations of their fathers, and daughters were taught what their mothers knew. The conscious discouragement of a critical independence of mind and the conservative values of Confucian training seemed suitable for the training of leaders. By the nineteenth century, however, the country was no longer stable. Pressures both internal and external were undermining traditional practices. By the final decades of the period a need was recognized for leaders who could think in new ways, solve problems never before faced, and apply new knowledge. By the 1840s shijuku . . .were providing practical training in various areas at an intermediate stage beyond Chinese studies. They had become agents of change from a traditional pattern of hereditary succession to a more modern function of schooling – the selecting and sorting out of students into occupational areas of ability and specialized training.

Such an exceptionally extensive and long established educational provision by the standards of the rest of Asia meant ingrained attitudes. General MacArthur and his well-meaning team did not just face an educational system created since the 1870s, but several hundred further years of educational thought and tradition. Not long after America had returned Japan to its independence in the 1950s Japan was hotly debating the teaching of ethics in schools. This was a fast return to the older traditions of Japanese schools. As a result the Ministry of Education issued an elementary school list of 36 moral virtues with a parallel list of 21 for lower secondary schools. An hour a week was to be devoted to teaching 'the virtues'. The list says much about the power of Japan's older educational traditions: The student is to revere his life, to promote his health, and to maintain his security; to become self-reliant, and not to depend on others; to make his dress, words and actions appropriate to the time and situation, and to be courteous; to keep his belongings in order to work for the beautification of his environment; to make the most of things and money and spend them efficiently; to make the best use of his time and lead a regular life; to respect the personalities not only of others but also of himself and promote mutual happiness; to state his opinions and behave according to his beliefs; not to be subject to others' opinions and actions blindly; to behave freely from his view and hope, and to be responsible for his actions; to be honest and faithful; to behave consistently with his whole heart; to love justice and hate injustice, and to resist temptation; to overcome all difficulties and to do everything throughout for the realisation of right aims; to reflect upon himself; to listen to others, to act deliberately; not to behave willfully; to lead an orderly life; to behave cheerfully with a bright and mild feeling; to care for animals and plants with a tender heart; to pay reverence to beauty and the divine; to have a pure heart; to know his own characteristics; to develop his merits; to do his best for higher aims and to have great hope; to act with rational judgement; to improve his life with creativity and imagination; to make an effort to inquire about the truth with the love of study; to try to do what he thinks reasonable and to go into new fields; to be kind to everyone; to take care of the weak and unfortunate; to respect and thank those who do their best for us and for the public;

to trust mutually and to help each other in a friendly fashion; to act impartially and to be fair to everybody; to understand others' positions and to be tolerant even of their mistakes with a broad heart; to understand the significance of rules and regulations which are made by the group and to observe them willingly; to insist on his rights and to carry out his duties; to recognise the reverence of labour and to work for the public in cooperation with others; to take good care of public property, to observe public morality and not to put others to trouble; to revere his family and to make his home better; to respect every person in the school and to build up a good reputation for the school; to have an ardent passion for the country with a self-consciousness as a Japanese and to make an effort towards the development of the nation as a member of international society; to have a proper understanding about world peoples and to keep on good terms with them (quoted by Tsugio Ajisaka, 'Moral Education in Japan', *Education in Japan*, volume III, 1968).

It is an exhaustive list which many British teachers would be happy to see followed by their charges. Although familiar Japanese themes are notably present the American Occupation priorities are also acknowledged. Perhaps, though, the major and obvious point is that the list came from Tokyo, not from the local board of education, or the PTA, or from individual teachers. The authority of the state in education is confirmed.

The Occupation's contribution to Japan's contemporary education system was substantial, but what always happens when change is imposed from an alien culture upon a central institution of long and distinguished standing is that the host country takes the first opportunity to revise the model to match familiar and highly prized traditions. Japan has a massive debt to the enlightenment of the Americans between 1945 and 1952, but has not been prepared to accept all of the latter's seemingly good ideas.

6 The Drive for Economic Great Power Status

The Japanese belief that they are a unique people of homogeneous culture, which today remains their greatest weakness, gave considerable advantages when the economy began to expand in the early post-American Occupation years. The decision to go for economic growth at virtually any cost demanded a commitment to what has been termed Japan Incorporated which would not have been possible to the same degree in most other countries. The emotional attachment to being Japanese, and thus not like other peoples, could be harnessed to national effort and economic achievement. Year after year in the 1960s Japan thus attained the unheard of economic growth of 10 per cent thereby doubling its economy every seven years or so. The education system reaffirmed Japanese sense of separateness and both supplied the right style of workers and confirmed and approved the national priority.

Kokichi Masuda in her paper 'Changing Japanese Mothers' (in *Non-formal Education for Women*, edited by Kazufusa Moro'oka, National Federation of Social Education of Japan, 1982) suggests that,

Looking back upon the past thirty years, it seems to be possible to divide them into three stages in order to understand the changes of Japanese society, the family, and the mothers. The first stage can be called that of the silent, fundamental change which started around 1955. This stage corresponds to the famous rapid economic growth in Japan. The impact of that growth upon the domestic setting was such as the Japanese had never before experienced. Certainly it did prepare the basis for the second stage. However, surprisingly enough, remarkable changes were invisible at least in terms of social problems in spite of the drastic economic changes. Irrespective of growing material affluence, people seemed to retain the traditional ways of life. The second stage, which began around 1965, was a really dramatic one just like an eruption of a volcano. The rapid progress of industrialization and urbanization at last brought explicit problems in political, economical and social aspects during this period. People began to notice the evil aspects

114

behind the material affluence. Many kinds of social issues such as the environmental pollution, women's liberation, anti-nuclear protests, students' unrest and others came out in public all at once. These movements were mainly supported by the young people, who were born just after the end of World War II, during the period of the baby boom. They were the bearers of new ideologies that ran against the traditional ways of life. Thus, the problem of the generation gap became visible and explicit in Japanese society. The third stage is from the mid-'70s to the present. This stage is characterized by the new conservatism and the emerging new social problems parallel with the tendency of highly industrialized countries. In other words, Japan was involved in international social problems usually observed in developed countries.

At the same Asian-South Pacific Bureau of Adult Education conference at which Kokichi Masuda gave her paper, Professor Kazuyo Yamamoto ('Women's Welfare and Social Participation') dealt with the standing of Japanese women and saw less change over the period from the 1950s to 1980s: 'One of the reasons for this unsatisfactory status lies in the traditional Japanese frame of concept, that is, men are supposed to work outside the home and women inside. This concept is still quite persistent, and has restricted the activities of many women. As a result, women themselves have a tendency to depend on men and to evade confronting the public and other situations of responsibility. Furthermore, women have not been given enough opportunities and experiences to train themselves socially, and consequently they lack social abilities and confidence'.

Women are in the majority in Japan and make the most important indicator of social change since the 1950s. Similarly, the world is aware of Japan's phenomenal economic growth, but other factors will be equally, if not more important to the Japanese and their culture. For example, in 1948 there were 198 946 kindergarten pupils, but in 1987 2 016 224; university students in 1948 numbered 11 978, but 1 934 483 in 1987; there were no junior colleges until 1950 when they had 15 098 students, but by 1987 there were 437 641; upper secondary schools in 1948 had 1 203 963 students and in 1987 5 375 107. Obviously such figures suggest a better educated population if only because the Japanese are in full-time education longer than the immediate postwar generation. With something like a third of the population beginning schooling at three years and ending at 22 a large proportion of the next generation of Japanese are, by international standards, highly educated. The Japanese belief in consensus makes such a privileged group conformist. During the period of rapid economic expansion such conformity was a major asset, particularly as Japan had good and cheap access to Western and notably American, industrial innovation. Without the latter, Japanese economic growth at the rates achieved would not have been possible. Japan owes much to such Western institutions as the Ma Bell Laboratories, or such more modest centres as the Chemistry Department of the University of Hull in England where liquid crystal was invented.

In 1955 Japan's share of the world's gross national product was 2 per cent. By 1980 it had reached almost 10 per cent, and by the end of the century it is expected to be 12 per cent. It is a dazzling performance. The leadership of such achievement has come virtually exclusively from graduates of the prestige universities. In every field in Japan it is almost impossible to be successful unless you obtain high scores throughout your schooling. The kyoiku mama (education mother) is committed to her child's school achievement for his or her economic life-chances. She will want her son to become Managing Director of Mitsubishi, a perfectly reasonable ambition in the meritocracy which is Japan, but that means an impeccable exam performance throughout childhood, youth, and early manhood. Japan is not a country of second-chances. Why should it be? The citizen is for the benefit of the state, not vice versa. This is part of the cost of a national state of mind which claims uniqueness for Japan, and thus grants exclusiveness to the citizen. Given such privileged membership, the citizen is expected to strive for the good of Japan. As ruthless examination competition will provide a more than adequate supply of very able candidates for the economy and national administration why waste resources and energy on the possibly bright student who stumbles, has other priorities, or drops out? Only Western individuality would have such illogical and self-indulgent ideas as second-chance education.

With a population of some 122 million people about 10 per cent of Japan's gross national product is involved in foreign trade. The make-up of the latter makes Japan's economy the most vulnerable of all the major states. It has to import over half of its food and 60 per cent of its energy comes from imports of oil. The Japanese recognised their dependence on imported raw materials before the Second World War and this inspired much of their military activity in Asia, plus the attempt to create a Greater East Asia Co-Prosperity

Sphere. Immediately after 1945 a combination of American aid, low living standards, and the modest performance of the Japanese economy made such vulnerability to the economic whims of the rest of the world less obvious. The drive for economic expansion brought home with a vengeance Japan's pressing need for good access to other people's resources. The brutal truth is that the world can cope without Japan, but Japan cannot cope without the rest of the world if its economy is to survive. The two rival super-economies of the United States and the European Economic Community could isolate themselves from the rest of the world with some economic discomfort, but no real hardship. To cut off Japan from the rest of the world would spell economic disaster. Japan's continuous international plea that it is economically more vulnerable than its major trading partners has much truth in it.

The success of the economy from the mid-1950s to the 1980s was not just in its rate of growth, but also in changing Japan's manufacturing image. Until well into the 1950s Japanese goods were seen as cheap and of inferior quality. Today the world buys such products because their quality and design are rarely matched elsewhere. This also brings its problems as it is the rich countries which can afford to buy such goods. Japan may see China as 1100 million consumers, but they have little buying power compared to the United States, Western Europe, or Australia. Half Japan's trade is with the affluent West, and most of the rest is made up of importing oil, food and raw materials. Rich countries trade mainly with rich countries, which is one of the many reasons why the European Economic Community will move quickly towards full political unity when such provincial politicians as Margaret Thatcher have left the stage. Britain's major trading partner is West Germany, not Africa, or China, or Latin America. Some 30 per cent of Japan's trade is with the United States. Its international vulnerability was harshly illustrated in 1973 when America, thinking its own needs would not be met, placed an embargo on the export of soya beans, which play a key role in Japan's diet. The more successful Japan's economy became during the 1960s and 1970s the more it was open to international influence and possible economic disaster. To survive as a stable nation Japan has to have an open and sympathetic world economic climate. The quadrupling, by the Organisation of Petroleum Exporting Countries, of the oil price in late 1973 produced notable inflation and economic crisis in Japan. Whilst the country handled the aftermath well, it could not cope with many such economic developments.

In discussing these issues with Professor Uesugi he made a number of important points: 'China wants to buy high-tech exports, but politically it is not easy for Japan to trade with China. Without trade, Japan cannot maintain herself. For example, in the Second World War Japan was shut out as a trading nation by America and Britain, and therefore tried to get its much needed raw materials from the South Pacific area. It is our most serious task to maintain good trade relationships. Since the later 1970s a lot of Japanese companies have built factories in Southeast Asia because of lower labour costs. Before the Second World War Japan gained her markets because of the cheap cost of her goods, but now her products are high in price. We must expect such manufacturers as Hong Kong, South Korea, and even China to produce many of the goods we now export, but at a lower price. Whilst we should not seek drastic change, we should change from building factories in foreign countries to being the economy which provides the rest of Asia with high technology'.

Besides an exceptionally well-educated and motivated workforce during the 1960s Japan's economic growth was greatly helped by easy access to Western markets, and notably that of the United States, whilst its own market saw a degree of protection. Whilst such domestic protectionism is declining in the face of increasingly vociferous foreign pressure, it was important when Japan was building up key industries to where they were competitive in international terms.

The bane of all Asian countries endeavouring to achieve economic growth, namely increase in population size, ceased to be a factor in Japan as industrial success mounted. Japan has limited growth in population which should stabilise at about 135 million early in the next century. To all intents and purposes Japan, like Western Europe, has a static population size, and the related problem of an ageing population structure. With rapid urbanisation after 1950 has come the two-child family encouraged by modest housing and the unique commitment to education. The Japanese hope their children will go to university, so rightly regard two children as the limit of what they can afford in terms of the financing of such education. Again, this is a contrast to the 1930s, when population growth was a major economic and social problem.

Political stability at home has been of crucial importance for Japan's economic achievement. Immediately after 1952 there were fears that the hostility between the left and right-wing political groups, particularly as the latter wished to 'clarify' the Emperor's role and to abandon treaty limitations on defence expenditure, might disrupt the country, but these proved ill-founded. Probably things reached a head in 1960 over the need to revise the Security Treaty with the United States. Whilst there were major demonstrations and some violence, the event was followed by a long period of political calm. In the later 1960s there were demonstrations over the American presence in Vietnam, and some nationalistic fervour arose over the continuing United States possession of Okinawa (returned to Japan in 1972). By 1970 only the GNP of America and the Soviet Union was greater than that of Japan. The balance of trade was to move dramatically in Japan's favour. In 1975 the advantage was still with the United States, but by the second half of the 1980s Japan's trade with America would show a $50 billion surplus. Such a state of affairs may be more ominous for Japan than the United States in the medium and long term. It is the sort of imbalance that might encourage economic isolationism in America.

Since 1945 Japan's relationship with the United States has been central to its economic development. In the early 1950s the Japanese began their growth momentum with the stimulation America's participation in the Korean War provided. American spending in Japan was substantial. Similarly, America's willingness to spend its taxes in providing military protection for Japan has permitted the latter to use perhaps 5 per cent of its GNP for more productive forms of investment. Nothing drains a country's resources more than investment in military forces and research. Japan was the most privileged of the major industrial states in not having to waste its money in such matters. Its so-called Self-Defence Forces have cost about 1 per cent of GNP. The Soviet Union and China during the period under review were using 10 per cent of their GNP on defence, whilst the American figure has usually been some 6 per cent. Investing a further 5 per cent of GNP in the economy and industrial research gives a country unique advantages in world markets. The increasing prosperity was matched by satisfaction amongst workers. Differences between the material well-being of the rural and urban areas declined, and, as has previously been noted, wages and salaries showed much less variation than in America or Western Europe.

Investment in the physical fabric of Japan did not keep up with its economic growth. The visitor to Japan is still made aware of the fact that it has put less money into roads and housing than is needed. A superb rail system helps to hide the fact that Japanese roads are notable only for their traffic-jams. In conversation with Professor Noriko Hiraki at the National Women's Education Centre it was pointed out to me that Japanese priorities have always been first clothes, then food, and only finally housing. This is in contrast to Britain, where housing has been a priority on any political party's agenda. That is changing. When noting a tipsy Japanese 'salaryman', impeccably dressed in regulation dark suit, white shirt and black shoes, urinating against the front of one of the most expensive prices of property in central Tokyo at about ten o'clock at night, I asked why he did not go home to his wife and family, which has always been my first priority. I had expected in reply to be told of the importance of the work group, the need to conform, to spend your evenings drinking as one of the boys, the confirmation of your place as part of the team which helps to make Sony, or Datsun, or Mitsui great. Instead I was informed, 'It is more fun to be out with the boys than cramped at home with a wife and two children in a tiny and inadequate apartment'. As more and more Japanese see how other affluent nations live, and are told of their overwhelming economic success and resulting personal affluence, the excuse that geography limits space and they must therefore live in small apartments will not be accepted. Foreign travel, as the tourist boom continues to grow or in line of work, not only broadens the mind, but makes the well-educated Japanese less tolerant of limitations in his own life style.

After it was published in 1872 Yukichi Fukuzawa's *An Encouragement of Learning* sold almost three and a half million copies. Its major message for the Japanese was that social mobility could be achieved through education. This gave added attraction to the Confucian traditions of respect for education inherited from an older Japan. Following 1945 Kojiro Kishimoto and Shigekazu Takemura ('Education in Japan after 1945', *Education in Japan*, volume 1, 1966) suggest three initial stages of educational development:

> The first stage covers the period of the allied occupation from 1945 to 1952, during which the educational system was drastically reformed through the democratization of Japan. A new Constitution was promulgated, new school laws were enacted and the present 6-3-3-4 school system was established. Teaching methods, school curricula, school administration and the system of teacher training were all greatly changed from the old ones, seeking to establish a democratic system of education. The second stage covers the period from 1952 to around 1957, during which revisional movements to meet the new situation were started by

the government, partly as a reaction against the reform of the occupation period, and partly as the adjustment to the new situation of the world. At first, even the revision of the school system was proposed by the Ordinance Review Committee, but it was met with a fierce opposition. But during this period, teaching methods, school curricula and school administration underwent certain modification, against which a vigorous campaign was embarked by the Teachers' Union. The political movement became the characteristic of Japan's Teachers' Union, and the antagonism between the Ministry of Education and the Teachers' Union caused confusion in the so-called new education. The third stage may be said to begin around 1958. This is the period in which enthusiastic movements for educational reform were started in many advanced countries of the world. Technological renovation in industry began to demand the development of human ability, for which the promotion of education among the people became indispensable. It was just at this period that the bulge of school population in post-war Japan came up to the upper secondary school level. Those who go on to the upper secondary schools after finishing the compulsory education increased greatly.

The withdrawal of the American Administration after 1952, and the further deterioration of Soviet-American relations during the Korean War (with the emergence of a hostile China under Mao Tse-tung), saw the launching of a revisional movement in education, as already mentioned. The conservatives attempted to re-establish the old order, with fierce opposition from the Teachers' Union. The Ordinance Review Committee, launched to re-examine the legislation passed under the Occupation, suggested reducing the number of universities, making junior colleges into vocational schools, dividing the lower secondary schools into two streams, only one of which would go onto the upper secondary schools, and shortening the period of compulsory education. These proposed measures to restrict educational opportunity were deeply unpopular. Although less than half the age cohort actually went on to the upper secondary schools, the figure was increasing rapidly. The measures were not implemented.

The Occupation decision to encourage a more democratic society by making social studies the core of all subjects were rejected. It was felt that moral education should be firmly introduced at the expense of social studies, as both the conservatives and many parents were

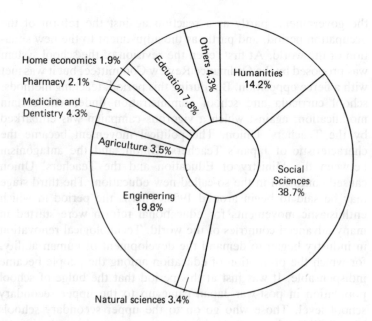

Home economics 1.9%
Pharmacy 2.1%
Medicine and
Dentistry 4.3%
Agriculture 3.5%
Engineering 19.8%
Natural sciences 3.4%
Education 7.8%
Others 4.3%
Humanities 14.2%
Social Sciences 38.7%

SOURCE Ministry of Education, *Outline of Education in Japan*, Tokyo 1987.

FIGURE 6.1 *Percentage Distribution of University Students by Major Field of Study, as of May 1985.*

worried about enough guidance being given in the schools. Similar fears concerning arithmetic and Japanese language standards, and whether children at secondary level were being exposed to adequate scientific and technical education to prepare them for work, led the Ministry of Education in 1958 to enlarge the subject teaching curriculum and make the new National Standards for the curricula mandatory, not advisory. As noted in the last chapter, the election of boards of education by the local community was ended. There had been many clashes between elected board members and local officials. The nomination of board of education members helped the Ministry of Education in its anxiety to re-establish its power over local education. In 1958 the Ministry of Education ordered the evaluation of teachers and in 1961 a nationwide achievement test for secondary students. The antagonism between the Teachers' Union and the Ministry of Education was firmly established.

In the 1960s the increasing popularity of higher secondary schools led to the development of a range of courses to match differing abilities and interests, such as favouring the humanities or wishing to study the sciences or technology. By 1965 over 70 per cent of the age cohort were attending upper secondary schools, although there was a difference between the urban and rural areas. This meant a need to review once more the curriculum, organisation and teaching methods of the schools. Of this development and its 1980s characteristics Professor Uesugi has commented:

There is great discontent with long school hours supplemented by juku (for a child having difficulty at school or with parents ambitious for them there are gakushu juku or private remedial tuition, and the examination crammer class called shingaku juku). Textbooks in schools have too much content, so not a few pupils do not master them easily or adequately. Drop-outs are not high in number, but in school many pupils do not master the content of a subject. Too many things are taught in too short a time. Of course, high talent responds well to such a system, but the average students lose their interest in study. In Britain half the 16-year-olds leave school (the minimum school-leaving age), but in Japan it is hard to find a reasonable job if you leave at 15. It thus becomes necessary to stay on to try to go to university in order to look good for the labour market. Before the Second World War 50% of the population worked in agriculture so academic success was not seen as important, but now white-collar jobs are the norm so the diploma is important. The one track system of secondary education has encouraged this as it is easy to move from the lower secondary school to the higher secondary school. After World War II the American belief in promoting the field of social studies to encourage democracy had its educational supporters. For example, the private universities found supplying social science places much cheaper than those for science with the costly laboratories and equipment (see Figure 6.1). However, companies favoured recruiting from departments of engineering, economics, or law. The conservative government wanted an education system which would identify high talent so it could then be placed in a hierarchical system in industry. Such tends to divide people, but enhances contested mobility. However, government attempts to increase vocational upper secondary schools were defeated by the parents who saw ordinary schools as the route to university. The conservative government likes the idea of cultivating vocational abilities in the young.

The remarkable growth of the Japanese economy in the 1960s finally destroyed the agrarian society with its deep commitment to conservatism and caste. The majority of the rural workforce moved to the cities. There was a rapid extension of the urban middle class, and increasing prosperity led to a levelling up of material well-being. Virtually all Japanese describe themselves as 'middle class', and this would seem a reasonable assessment. The extended family has virtually disappeared, and thus the underpinning organisation for commitment to filial devotion and family good name.

The economic successes of Japan brought with them, as in other countries, a new materialism. The old stability of knowing one's place in society and knowing that it would be unchanging ended in the 1960s and 1970s. New stabilities have been sought to replace some fo the certainties of the past. The explosion in demand for education is a significant part of that search. Fukuzawa's message of 1872 that education equals social mobility became engrained in the Japanese soul. Those who flocked in from the rural areas in the 1950s and 1960s, and the greatly expanded new middle class, looked to education, and notably higher education, to enable their children to be confirmed in the new affluence and to do even better than they had.

As a result of the Japanese commitment to education the highly centralised system has made demands upon students which would be thought unacceptable in many other developed countries. The Japanese pupil faces a longer school day than the British, and still has a five and a half day week, though Saturday classes are ending in the universities. The summer holidays are barely more than a month, with a short vacation in the New Year, and just before the start of the school year at the beginning of April. School discipline is well established, and homework begins in the first year of the primary school. Despite very similar performances, schools are assessed by parents on their students' results, and there is a clear pecking order. Probably half of pupils of lower secondary schools attend a juku at some time. Japan is a closely organised society, and education determines status. To the Japanese Margaret Thatcher's often romantic view of the self-made man or woman would seem largely irrelevant. Such people do exist in Japan, but they are the exception and often of an older generation. In fact, Britain is tending to be increasingly like Japan in such matters. The Japanese note that amongst prime ministers only Tanaka Kakuei was not a university graduate, but since 1945 only James Callaghan amongst British premiers did not attend university.

Merry White notes (p.49), 'The reason why Japanese industry works and why Japanese schools teach, why workers don't quit and why children don't drop out of school, is that what is most wanted out of life – stability, security and support – are acquired through effort and commitment. This lesson is taught to the young, at home and at school'. In inculcating such a lesson the mother is seen as the key influence, and schools rely on her availability and full support. A child dependent on his mother is regarded as a healthy relationship, which is quite contrary to British practice. The parents will assume their child has the capacity to succeed at school, and that the mother's total effort will be employed alongside to help that to happen.

The decision in the 1940s to greatly extend the number of universities put an end to higher education being seen as for an élite only, but did establish certain institutions, such as the Universities of Tokyo and Kyoto, as the élite establishments. Since the 1950s competition for places at the top universities has increased dramatically. This leads to what has been called Japan's 'examination hell'. After such gigantic effort many undergraduates are, inevitably, disappointed with the intellectual experience of university.

In an editorial in the *Mainichi Daily News* of 28 March 1989 entitled 'High Cost of Education' it was pointed out that

The average payment made during the initial year to private universities has gone over one million yen for the first time'. The editorial continued, 'If university tuition becomes too expensive, the opportunity for young people to go to university is bound to show a big difference, depending on the economic conditions of the respective households. This raises two questions. First is whether the concept of equal opportunity for education ends at the compulsory education level. In order to advance to a university, an aspirant must first graduate from a senior high school. Even in the case of public senior high schools, a considerable amount of money will be required for preparatory school study. The reality is that the children of families that are less favoured economically are not assured equal opportunity for education. In order to take a university entrance examination, further study at a preparatory school is often necessary, entailing more expense. Furthermore, even in the case of public schools today, the burden of payments that students must make has about reached the maximum level that most households can bear . . . . The second question is whether it is proper to determine that a university's tuition fee must be borne entirely by the parents. On the other hand, if the state is to assist, a huge amount of money must be poured into universities. Since there is a limit to public funds, it will become difficult to establish new universities. Moreover, if state finances become constricted, subsidies to private schools are reduced. After such subsidies were cut 10 per cent in 1984, the amount has been moved sideways or raised only slightly since fiscal 1985. During this period the number of those desiring to attend universities increased and new universities were founded. This caused the percentage of subsidies to drop, as far as the universities were concerned, and led to an increase in payments to be made by the students. A large amount of government money is going to state universities. Even in the case of other universities, the tuition should inherently be low. It was so at one time. The first-year payment was about half of a university graduate's first-month's salary. Today it is far beyond the salary of an office worker nearing retirement. American universities are also raising tuitions. But state universities there have much larger student capacities than private schools. There are many endowments and, in turn, many scholarships. The concept of higher education for as many as possible has not been lost. A university should not be a place for only a limited number of students. It is true that the criticism exists that universities have tuned into a 'leisure land' and that students are losing the incentive to study. This is not the responsibility of the students alone. Universities should not become a place only for those who come from well-to-do families. That would not be beneficial for Japanese society as a whole. Greater thought should be given to the administration of higher education.

As an editorial it says much about Japanese society, its education system and, obviously, higher education. Education is the vehicle for achieving a good job, and therefore families will make great financial sacrifices to aid their children in educational success. Such success is symbolised in getting into university. If the prestige (and cheaper) state universities reject your child, then the money must be found for tuition at one of the more numerous private universities. Should the government be doing more in the way of financial help? The commitment to a world of educational opportunity for all makes a reassuring theme in a society where democracy has only firmly taken root since 1945. Finally, Japanese unease about the quality of provision within universities, and the attendant belief that students waste their time as undergraduates persists. In a country of virtually unparalleled wealth it is surprising to the visitor that government funding of higher education is so relatively modest, and the reputed quality of university provision often below that which the Japanese would tolerate in other walks of life. As early as 1971 Nagai Michio stated in his book *Higher Education in Japan: Its Take-off and Crash* (University of Tokyo Press): 'During my years as a university professor in Japan I have been preoccupied with the state of higher education in that country. The content of education is meagre and research that has gained world recognition is sparse in proportion to the number of institutions and students. Faculties are dominated by academic cliques; planning for research and education is wanting. In short, glaring deficiencies are far too numerous'.

To those of us who have seen the PhD degree become the union card in British universities, as it had a generation before in American institutions of higher education, and noted the way German top management has doctoral degrees, it is a surprise to find that Japan since the Occupation has established a different norm. The PhD degree seems relatively unimportant. Government departments and industry recruit the graduates of the prestige universities and then provide the equivalent of in-house postgraduate training. Notably in the humanities and social science faculties, where completing a PhD programme seems to take an interminably long time, a majority of the professors do not have a doctoral degree (often the PhD in Japan has a different title such as Doctor of Law).

The universities' poor research record compared to, say, British universities is again the result of the evolution of a different tradition. Business and government see themselves as even more deeply involved in research than their British equivalents, so much of the work which might be done in British university laboratories is undertaken in company facilities. And what is a grossly underfunded university system, notably in the larger private sector, inevitably concentrates on teaching because research is always an expensive business. Japan has gone for a mass higher education system, but less than half its cost is met from government sources, either national or local.

Underfunding not only means a weak research tradition in a

university, but also large classes and little contact with the academic staff. Much is said of the reputation of Japanese education resting on the well taught primary and secondary school system. Certainly higher education to the visitor looks disappointing in quality except for the famous former Imperial universities and the very best of the private universities, such as Waseda and Keio.

The Japanese worry about their poor research record and their reliance on Western innovation. There are numerous initiatives to counter this, such as Tsukuba Science City in Ibaraki Prefecture which is aimed at research in the natural sciences and was opened in 1985. As I am writing this in the University of Kyoto it would seem pertinent to describe a little of the 16 000 hectare Kansai Science City, which is being built between Kyoto, Osaka and Nara on Keihanna Hill off Route 163. The most notable complex so far belongs to the Advanced Telecommunications Research Institute set up with both government and private money to research auditory and visual perception, communication systems, interpreting telephony, and optical and radio communication. The Institute is designed to accommodate up to 200 researchers, and it is intended these should include scientists from Europe and North America.

In Kansai Science City the aim is to modify what is seen as Japan's too rigid approach to research, to be willing to let scientists pursue a line of work even when the practical outcomes are not obvious. Shoichiro Kobayashi, Director General of the Kansai Research Institute, was reported as saying (*Japan Times*, 11 April 1989) that the project was to break away from Japan being accused of getting a 'free ride on basic technologies developed overseas'. The City will include the International Institute for Advanced Studies, a proposal of a former President of Kyoto University, Azuma Okuda, who persuaded private companies to donate over four billion yen. Its building will be ready in the early 1990s. Although the Tsukuba Science City was a national project, the Kansai Science City is privately funded. The International Institute for Advanced Studies will develop new areas of science and invite leading scholars in a particular field from around the world to make up the research team. Work has begun on the building for a 7.8 billion yen Ion Engineering Institute, a field in which Japan does have an international reputation. The Kansai Science City is expected to link in with existing universities in the area and Japan's first all-graduate programme Advanced Science Technology Institute planned for Takayama district in Nara Prefecture. The

Kansai Science City will be completed early in the next century.

Although the existing universities may get some spin-off from the development of high-investment Science Cities, it is something of a commentary on the differing tradition to that of the West European and North American research approach which developed during the period of Japan's economic take-off. Applied research was used in the companies and based on overseas innovation, and provided a singularly rewarding underpinning for fast industrial and commercial expansion. The universities were primarily to select the brightest and the best candidates for the economy and to act as teaching institutions, although for industry and the government recruiters this was a secondary consideration.

The United States is no longer willing to make freely available to Japan the results of its research, and Western Europe is less convinced of the modern relevance of the old belief that knowledge is international. As mentioned frequently, Japan's unique economic growth of the last 30 to 40 years was based on its own native qualities, but also on full access to one of the most brilliantly creative periods of American and European Science. Unlike the 1960s and 1970s, America and Western Europe now treat Japan as a very serious economic competitor so it has to establish a world class research tradition which has not been necessary previously.

Reischauer sums up the problem (p.200):

> The Japanese are often accused of being intellectually not very creative, and this weakness is commonly attributed at least in part to the inadequacies of their university system, though more obvious culprits would be the tendency toward rote memory work in earlier education and the whole conformist nature of their society. No one can doubt that the Japanese have great artistic creativeness, but their achievements in the realms of science and philosophy do seem less impressive. No modern Japanese thinker has appeared noteworthy to the rest of the world – though we should remember the language barrier is probably in part responsible for this. Japanese have made relatively few contributions to basic science, and only a few have been singled out for Nobel Prizes. Japanese industrial triumphs have been based largely on efficient borrowing or ingenious adaptations of foreign technology rather than on independent scientific discoveries. Political thought, philosophy and scholarship in the social sciences are to a large extent the reworking or synthesis of ideas derived

from abroad, rather than original creative work . . . Japanese
have always seemed to lean more toward intuition rather than
toward reason, to subtlety and sensitivity in expression rather than
to clarity of analysis, to pragmatism rather than to theory, and
to organizational skills rather than to great intellectual concepts.
They have never set much store by clarity of verbal analysis and
originality of thought.

Of course, it is worth reminding ourselves that a similar review
could have been made of American science prior to the 1940s; it
was largely dependent on borrowing from Europe. It is since the
Second World War that the research work in the United States has
established its international leadership. As with all dynamic societies
Japan is changing, as it has to change to accommodate new realities.
All people are similar, despite the deceptive veneer which cultural
variety presents. If it is a priority, as it must be for a Japan in a less
sympathetic world, then it will develop scientific creativity.

As already mentioned there are education barriers in the way,
many of them inherited from the 1960s and the rapid expansion
of the economy. The junior and senior high schools expanded to
meet demand under strong central government direction. As part
of a national obsession with job selection there was extraordinary
competition for places at a small number of famous upper secondary
schools. Similarly, the whole upper secondary school system became
geared to high performance in entrance examination scores to gain
places at the more highly regarded universities. Such priorities led
to ruthless standardisation, reinforced by the use of juku to achieve
even higher conventional performance. Those who cannot keep up
are thought to be increasing in number. As the Prime Minister's
Office's National Assembly for Youth Development reported in
March 1988 (*The Rising Generation in Japan*), 'A majority (two
thirds) of children at elementary and lower secondary school say
they understand what is taught in class. However, there are quite a
few who do not understand classes well enough. Many elementary
school children take some lessons outside school, mainly learning
some art skills. Nearly half of lower secondary school students go
to tutoring classes to supplement their school learning. Nearly half of
upper secondary school students feel dissatisfied with their school'.

Long hours of schooling, often typified by drill and rote learning,
may have brought benefits to the economy in the 1960s and 1970s,
but at a cost. Japanese children were found to exercise less frequently

than their American or European counterparts with some disadvantage to physical growth. Already we have seen that schooling Japanese style may not encourage the enquiring mind even if it does produce a well disciplined work force. Even the resulting strong commitment to the group can bring high costs as well as rewards. Mr Saito, Director General of the Life-long Education Division of the Ministry, was moved from that key post in April 1989 when his superior Vice-Minister of Education Kunio Takaishi was found to be involved in the Recruit scandal. He was innocent of any association with the Recruit débâcle, but the dishonour of his chief saw the Minister of Education moving out all the Department of Education's associated top people. One bad apple sees the rest of the fruit shifted out too.

A reinforcing factor for many of the above discussed characteristics of Japanese education during the period from 1955 onwards was the nature of the Japanese language and the debate about how it should be taught in school. Probably the language included dialects of Korean, but over many centuries it has borrowed heavily from other sources such as Chinese to turn itself into a mongrel, but distinct, language in much the same way that English has evolved. The Japanese got their form of writing from the Chinese which they modified with two phonetic systems. It is a complex and difficult form of writing which demands much rote work to master. A Latin script would be ideal for the Japanese language, but tradition dies hard. The schools' inclination to favour memory work is encouraged by a written language which demands rote work.

Efforts to make Japanese language teaching less deadening were introduced during the Occupation. In 1946 came the Modern Kana (the 2000 or so Chinese characters are called kanji, whilst the two phonetic systems are hiragana and katakana, which gives the total writing system the name kana) Orthography Act which aimed at limiting the number of characters in every-day use. In the Ministry of Education reforms of 1947 the Japanese language (and also mathematics) were made 'tool' subjects with the former including grammar, spelling, reading, writing, speaking and listening skills. Before the Second World War some 2000 Chinese characters had to be learned in elementary school. The new figure was 996 to be mastered in the primary school and 400 in secondary school. Prewar Japanese language education had been based on tuition in grammar and the Japanese classics, whilst the new system aimed to give children a better working knowledge that they could use in their daily lives. This challenged the teaching of, notably, the period of Military Government when the Japanese language was bound up with a mystique of ultranationalism.

The end of the Occupation saw a conservative reaction over the teaching of Japanese language reforms. The disruption of the War and its aftermath saw a fall in the academic performance of children in all subjects, but declining literacy became a central issue. The number of Chinese characters to be taught was increased by the Minister of Education. As Professor Toshio Nakauchi (*The Modernization of Japanese Education*, volume II) notes, 'The private sector began making recommendations for the new direction of language education. One theory stressed the importance of retaining individuality in the Japanese language, as well as acquiring a higher level of linguistic skill, while others contended that language education should emphasize talents that would serve to uphold the foundations of the language. Some also insisted on the importance of grammar education, which, in a certain sense, had been neglected as merely part of reading training. Still others advocated the reintroduction of the three-stage reading method systematised before the war, and, as an alternative, some proposed a teaching method called 'one-stage comprehensive reading'. Some urged that literature be separated from Japanese language education'. The debate might be wide and vigorous, but an increasingly old-style Ministry and a buoyant, but instinctively conservative, business community (the old alliance of government and industry) returned the teaching of the Japanese language to the deeply-rooted prewar methods of rote learning. The explosion in demand for post-compulsory education in the 1960s reinforced the trend. The high level of competition for places in the more favoured secondary schools saw the re-emergence of the dominant role of the Japanese classics and the learning of prewar-style complex grammar.

Prewar education at secondary level had been for the privileged of the rural areas and the city-dwelling middle class. In the expansion of the 1960s it was taken over by the urban working class and the children of farmers. Whilst such a development was much to be encouraged it did give further support to a system which suggested the rote-learning was the best way to get the newcomers through examinations. For all its many good points the teaching of Japanese language in schools had done little to directly affect and enrich the day-to-day lives of the citizenry. But that was not necessarily the first priority of the Department of Education and of Japanese industry in the 1960s and 1970s.

The Japanese education system produces people of great charm with much sensitivity to those they work with, good at fitting-in. They are hard-working, after schooling which was largely a hard-slog, and have what might be termed 'stickability'. When I visited the delightful Yoshimori Suzuki of the Education Division of the National Diet Library I thought I had at last found an organisation which would not deliver precisely what I asked for. I was seeking a number of early Department of Education papers such as that prepared for the Louisiana Purchase Exposition in 1904. Initially Mr Suzuki drew a blank, but then his energy became impressive and from various parts of that large collection everything I asked for arrived. It left us with time to discuss the 1988 Education Reform Act in Westminster which Mr Suzuki was carefully studying. I was a resource to employ in such thorough analysis of another country's legislation. I wondered if anyone in the House of Commons Library reviewed the Diet's education debates.

In contrast, a school system which is conservative in its methods and objectives can produce workers overly wedded to old ways. I have frequently found Japanese bureaucracy slow in its methods. To take a small incident as trivial evidence: in England I bought Fuji Bank travellers' cheques (in yen). In Kyoto at a large and far from overworked branch of the Fuji Bank from the time I handed over the travellers' cheques with the relevant small form until I received the banknotes took 47 minutes. The Royal Bank of Scotland (Chorley branch) could teach Fuji a thing or two.

It is necessary for Europeans and Americans to marvel and enjoy the Japanese economic achievement, but not to assume that the way the Japanese do things is always suited to British, or American, or French practice. For example, the Japanese school system which expanded enormously during the 1960s and 1970s had, as we have noted, a number of limitations which it would be unwise to copy.

The development of social education programmes for women during the postwar period has illustrated Japanese good intentions and some fine provisions. The Ministry of Education, Science and Culture's *Women and Education in Japan* (Tokyo, 1986) contains much information on what has developed since the passing of the 1949 Social Education Law. In a country which during the 1960s and 1970s has been dominated by the needs of the economy, 'women' and 'social education' were often seen as secondary to 'men' and 'vocational training', and therefore say much about Japanese attitudes in education. A visit to Teruko Ohno, Director of the Women's Education Division of the Ministry's Life-long Learning Bureau, does much to reassure the doubting Westerner that the government is intent on improving the status of women. Besides such obvious symbols as the National Women's Education Centre, the Ministry has been involved in programmes of data collection and information dissemination with research projects to generate new knowledge and affect policy. On my visit to Teruko Ohno in 1989 I was given a report on the role of fathers in the United States, West Germany and Japan which is very revealing regarding differences in parenting. The Ministry also subsidises women's social education courses at local boards of education level and helps education associations with programmes of women's and/or parents' education.

Since the 1949 Act, and notably from the time of the United Nation's Decade for Women which ended in 1985, and in which the Japanese government produced a National Plan of Action to improve the standing of Japanese women, educational opportunities for women have improved. Japan remains a man's world, but less so than it was in the 1970s. In 1977 the first edition of *Feminist* was published, and Japanese scholars formed the International Group for Study on Women. In 1979 came The Women's Studies Association of Japan. The first Chair of Women's Studies had been established at Tokyo Women's College in the 1960s; by 1987 128 universities and junior colleges had women's studies programmes. As Professor Makoto Yamaguchi notes (*Feminism and Adult Education in Japan*, June 1988), 'With the ratification of the United Nations Convention on the Elimination of All Forms of Discrimination Against Women, Japanese women have been participating slowly but steadily in the political decision-making at all levels. In this situation the question is women's ability in these activities: decision-making, management, leadership and group-forming. As most of those who take part in decision-making were men, the programme in adult education for women to learn about decision-making must be developed. There is no accumulation of such learning nor exchange of information and experience in those activities'.

Aided by the government, systematic programmes of 'Women's Classes' have developed nationally, and numbered 34 000 in 1984 and 1.53 million participants. Each course was up to 30 hours with home management, hobbies, education and vocational guidance popular subjects. In 1985 the Ministry started study courses on women's issues to challenge the passive role of women in Japanese society. In 1986 to this initiative was added preparatory seminars for women wishing to return to work. In the cities in particular many private enterprises have developed social education courses aimed at women. These often have a strong similarity to the programmes put on by local education authorities in Britain, but the fee is high by such British adult education standards. A visit to such a programme based in an Osaka department store in 1988 suggested charges up to six times that of my home adult education centre for a similar course. Private enterprise is usually about making a profit, whether it is selling shoes, surgery or adult education.

A number of boards of education and women's organisations began in the 1970s offering leadership training courses. In 1984 programmes to help women become involved in voluntary activities numbered 212 (9100 women). The latter are aimed at encouraging women's social participation to the benefit of the community through helping with day-care, work with the elderly and handicapped, aiding environmental issues, and reading guidance for children.

The period of rapid economic growth saw increasing interest in parent education. These are usually organised by the local boards of education and in 1984 numbered 23 000 classes with 1.6 million members. From 1981 classes for prospective parents (newly-weds and pregnant women) were launched with considerable success (50 000 students in the first year). The increase in married women working in 1986 led the Ministry to start parent education courses for two-income families. Encouraged by the Ministry 41 out of 47 prefectures now offer Parent Education Guidance Programmes to deal with young mothers' questions about child-rearing and educa-tion. In 1984 530 000 young couples used the service.

Subsidised by the Ministry in 1984 44 prefectures offered an integrated programme on family education, aimed at parental under-standing and guidance of their children. This includes a telephone service for consultation. There is also a weekly television programme on parent education. The kominkans (citizens' public halls) numb-ered 17 520 in 1984 and held 83 000 classes for adults. Some 4.2 million people attended, of whom 67 per cent were women. Of such programmes Professor Yamaguchi states, 'Not only in school edu-cation, but also in adult education, administrators and practitioners are men, and those who are led are women. How much knowledge and insight do those man-leaders have in regard to women's issues and problems that women are faced with and have to solve through learning?' The same point could be made of British adult education.

Another growth area in adult education is that of classes for those over 65 years of age aimed at keeping up the interest of the older citizen in society and helping them to lead mentally and physically active lives. In 1983 there were 25 000 such classes with 1.8 million students, of whom 56 per cent were women.

In our many conversations Professor Uesugi had said that, 'Social education aims at improving living conditions through learning, so it is imperative that the Japanese adult educator researches and studies such living conditions. Whilst non-vocational adult education is popular in Japan, the British tradition of liberal adult education is not so powerful. The government would like to extend vocational adult education'. In 1984 some 308 public and private universities offerd 2 162 extension courses attended by a quarter of a million people (50 per cent women).

In 1985 the University of the Air began to admit students. It was launched with a single Faculty of Liberal Arts. Like the Open University, it uses printed course materials sent to the student by post, supplemented by radio and television broadcasts (see Figure 6.2). The University registered 17 000 students in its first year from a wide range of ages and occupations. Other correspondence courses are created mainly by non-profit organisations. In 1986 the Ministry authorised 169 such courses from 42 organisations and 195 000 students enrolled (25.7 per cent women). Of the men students 89.8 per cent were pursuing technical courses, whilst 57.8 per cent of the women studied domestic and cultural subjects.

Besides the National Women's Education Centre, which provides an intellectual leadership for the fight to improve the standing of Japanese women, there are 111 public and private women's centres offering training, exchanges and information services, and various activities for women's groups. The National Women's Education Centre has an important training and research commitment, for example, about a hundred Japanese women each year participate in its Advanced Course for Leaders of Women's Education. In 1988 a four-year project was launched by the Centre to promote women's participation in society. This saw a research committee established to provide guidelines for a research programme to be carried out in the second and third years with resulting plans available for action in the fourth year. In the period from September to November of 1988 a second project in cooperation with Ochanomizu University saw researchers visiting organisations and groups in Belgium, England, France, Italy, The Netherlands and West Germany to explore women's studies opportunities in Europe. The Centre has a key role in disseminating information in Japan on national and international ideas and activities. Since it opened in 1977 some 850 000 people have used the Centre.

Other initiatives have been taken to make the Occupation ambition of a more democratic and broader-based educational service effective. In 1965 the National Education Centre of the Institute of Social Education Training was set up. From 1963 the Ministry of Education, Science and Culture has been notably active in promoting policies aimed at improving the position of women. In 1976 it began a long-term project to encourage women's volunteer activities.

The largest women's organisations are the National Federation of Regional Women's Organisations (Zenkoku-Chiikifujindantai-Renrakukyogikai) with six million members, the National Federation of Mothers' Associations for Safety Traffic (Zenkoku-Kotsuanzen-Hahanokai-Rengokai) with 5 824 140 members, and the National Women's Association of Agricultural Cooperation (Zenkoku-Nokyo-Fujin-Soshiki-Kyogikai) with 2 603 522 members. There are numerous other women's groupings ranging from the 692 members of the National Association of Women Inventors (Zenkoku-Hatsumei-Fujin-Renmei) to the 270 members of the Society of Japanese Women Scientists (Nihon-Fujin-Kagakusha-no-Kai), all of which suggests a healthy democracy and some progress over the period of the last three decades towards a more equal society. But women suffer severe job discrimination, less freedom in marriage than their husbands, and carry most of the responsibility for the family. The Ministry of Labour's slogan for 1989 was 'Changing Women, Changing Men and Changing Society'. Men have had to make during the years of expanding the economy a total commitment to their companies at the expense of their family life. The firm has been their life. On retirement many wives have referred to their husbands as a 'wet fallen leaf' or 'industrial waste'. As Japan is now less obsessive over economic performance this is beginning to move 'the family' centre stage. Great social changes will inevitably follow, but a woman's inability to get a good job after marriage will keep the divorce rate low. There are also dangers in underestimating the degree of satisfaction many women get from their present dominant role within the family.

The position of women in Japanese society is closely allied to the health of democracy in the country. A conforming society

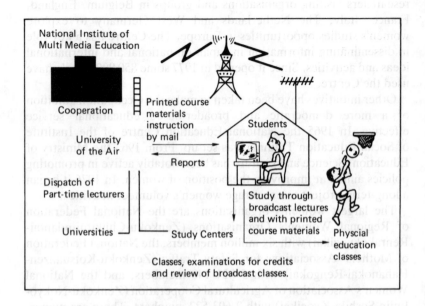

National Institute of
Multi Media Education

Cooperation

Printed course
materials
instruction
by mail

University
of the Air

Students

Reports

Dispatch of
Part-time lecturers

Study through
broadcast lectures
and with printed
course materials

Universities

Study Centers

Physical
education
classes

Classes, examinations for credits
and review of broadcast classes.

SOURCE Ministry of Education, Science and Culture, *Education in Japan*, Tokyo 1986.

FIGURE 6.2 *System of Instruction at the University of the Air*

can endanger the well-being of democratic institutions. And yet, with India, Japan would seem the great triumph of democracy's extension since 1945. Nobody expects Japan to return to military or despotic government but, like Britain during the 1980s, there are worrying signs. During the Recruit scandal in 1989 Michio Watanabe, Chairman of the Liberal Democratic Party's Policy Affairs Research Council, was one of a number of people making high-handed statements when he declared, 'There are a large number of Liberal Democratic Party Diet members, so it can't be helped if there is some corruption among them. The opposition parties are guard dogs and should be allowed to bark from time to time'. That sounded like the statement of a man who believes in a one party state.

The Japanese have been interested in ethics since at least Prince Shotoku's 17-article Constitution of 604 AD. During the rapid industrialisation of the 1960s there was a feeling that the increase in urbanisation and phenomenal growth in the economy had produced a more self-centred people. The social conformity demanded of the individual, however strong his or her self-identity, often produced social rebellion of a particularly extreme and unpleasant type such as the Sekigun (Red Army) killings of the period of hectic economic expansion.

In 1966 the Ministry of Education's Central Education Council published its advisory paper, 'The Image of the Ideal Japanese'. It stated, 'The postwar economic recovery in Japan is internationally regarded as a wonder. With the economy blooming, however, some people have adopted egotistic and epicurean attitudes. Meanwhile, there is still a feeling of spiritual hollowness and unrest left over from defeat in the war. If this condition of growing materialistic desire and spiritual emptiness endures, we cannot hope for long-term economic prosperity or a truly improved quality of life. Industrialization of Japan requires the development of human ability and at the same time, the improvement of humanity, because the development of human ability will lose its very base without an improvement of humanity, eventually reducing man to a mere producer/consumer'. (Quoted by Professor Toshihiko Saito, *The Modernization of Japanese Education*, volume II). The Council called for 'the cultivation of ethical consciousness' which began to look suspiciously like a plea to return to prewar patriotism. A debate raged around the paper with one group making a strong plea to nurture human rights rather than consciousness of duties and obligations. It was suggested that the Japanese had yet to take seriously such concepts as equality and freedom.

The policy of the 1960s of growth at any cost brought with it problems of atrocious environmental pollution, higher crime rates, a rise in violence against teachers and parents, and increased bullying in schools. Often the figures look modest by American, or even West European, standards, but they worried the Japanese. In 1971 Professor Shozen Shibano wrote in the British journal *Youth* ('Youth Service Japanese Style'),

Generation conflicts are common all over the world. Especially in Japan youth find it difficult to become adults themselves in the traditionally established manner. What was peculiar to Japan was the loss of confidence on the part of parents whose tradition was discredited after the defeat of the country. In addition the sudden democratisation emphasised the emancipation of ego. The so-called soft-education of the American type was combined with this trend. It is only natural that the strong individualistic quality has not been formed among children of the postwar period. Moreover youth today are exposed to difficulties in rapid social change. This is the critical situation which produces radical student dissent and acts of vandalism.

Beginning in 1978 Japan started to tackle successfully its awesome pollution problems, but has found more difficult other factors which limit the quality of life such as the overcrowding in the rapidly expanded cities. However, as in Britain and other European states, what Japan has called kogai (public injury) issues are firmly on the national agenda.

During the 1980s the Prime Minister's Office set up a Management and Coordination Agency with a Youth Affairs Administration within it. Twelve of the ministries and government agencies also established youth departments. The resulting National Assembly for Youth Development booklet 'The Rising Generation in Japan', already mentioned and published in March 1988, shows much enlightened thinking in dealing with the future, and the problems inherited from the period of rapid growth of the 1960s and 1970s. The figures given are for 1986 and show that there were 185 373 juvenile criminals between the ages of 14 and 20, and that 52.3 per cent were 14 and 15 year olds. There were 979 cases of violence in lower secondary schools, and 314 in upper secondary schools. Police were called to 845 cases of hazing. There were 856 cases of in-family violence, with the mother the most likely victim. Eight hundred and two young people committed suicide.

In response the government has listed various proposals in the pamphlet. On school education it intends to improve kindergarten facilities so that all four to five year olds who wish to go are able to. A committee investigated problematic behaviour in school pupils and made recommendations to end such developments as hazing. Compulsory education at primary and lower secondary level is to be improved. Higher education is to see its quality and variety developed, with new ideas like the University of the Air expanded. Japanese children abroad are to have 80 schools full-fledge and 112 supplementary schools. To aid returnees help will be given to assimilate them. This last point will make much of the brochure seem cock-eyed to Western readers as the uniquely insular Japanese are busy proclaiming 'internationalism'. If Japan is genuinely internationally minded it is legitimate to ask why children greatly enriched by foreign experience have so much trouble in being accepted back in Japanese schools? Is it that for all their politeness to foreigners the Japanese only feel easy and trusting of other Japanese? When I was young my great aunts, brought up in Plymouth in the latter part of the Victorian Age, had a similar view of those who were not British. Their manners were always impeccable but foreigners, well, poor things, were just not British. Two World Wars and, more importantly, the arrival of mass foreign travel have made the British less insular, although the football hooligan shows how far we have yet to progress. The Japanese face the bigger challenge of dismantling the myth of their cultural and racial homogeneity. In 1987 1 032 000 young people between the ages of 15 and 24 travelled abroad. Such travel by the most open minded of age groups will produce change. But economic success can, and almost always does, produce feelings of superiority. The education system, invariably drawn into national policies to sustain economic success, may also fuel nationalism and an attendant feeling of 'being different'.

Those exploring any genuine differences between the Japanese and Europeans or North Americans frequently mention 'amae'. The distinguished Japanese medic Takeo Doi made the concept well known in the West through his book *The Anatomy of Dependence*. Amae is to look to others for love and approval. The British mother's desire to make her child 'stand on his or her own two feet', as noted previously, contrasts with the Japanese mother's belief in giving her child constant attention. Merry White notes that for the Japanese, 'To perform well in school and other settings is important, but that is mostly regarded as a visible demonstration of a capacity to be a good (social) person. Americans, by contrast, tend to give much higher priority to individual skills and attributes, "independence" key among them, and to see one's interpersonal skills as more superficial – "social graces", a means rather than an end' (p.23). The tradition of amae implies in adulthood the seeking of approval for one's actions from others. This gives to the group powerful sanctions against those defiant of group norms and priorities. Of course, as in all such sweeping statements on differences between the Japanese and others there are dangers in assuming a larger gulf than actually exists. For others also belong to groups, such as those at work, and seek the approval of colleagues. It is important to establish such facts as that Samuel Smiles' *Self-Help* was as much a bestseller in nineteenth-century Japan as in Europe and North America after it was published in 1859.

The changes of the 1960s and 1970s have been enormous in social terms. Like Britain, Japan is now a highly urbanised society typified by the nuclear family. Because the latter is a relatively recent development perhaps there remains some vestige of the extended family in a way that is no longer true in Britain, but old, rurally sustained, customs are either gone or declining fast in importance. Differences of degree remain, but Japan is increasingly notable for its similarity to Europe and North America.

The most notable of all developments in the history of humankind, as against the comparable innovation of the development of agriculture in prehistory, was the Industrial Revolution with its replacement of human muscle by mechanical power. In all countries affected by such dramatic change people switched from being at least 80 per cent rural living to over 90 per cent city dwelling. Such social change has only one equivalent in the record of people and that is from being wandering hunters and gatherers to settled farming communities. These industrial changes took place in Britain up to 200 years ago, whilst the move to the cities in Japan was still vigorously in progress during the 1960s. Such all-transforming developments inevitably mean the old ways remain important and deeply influential for some time. America began its industrialisation in Massachusetts in the 1820s, but in the later 1940s tried to translate over a century of resulting change to the education system of a Japan still 40 per cent or more rurally based. The reaction to the American inspired innovation which followed in the 1950s was predictable. What was surprising was that so much of the educational change of the 1940s was found acceptable and popular.

The social changes during the period of rapid economic growth from the late 1950s to the 1980s were substantial. Again, it is worth mentioning how much more leisurely was such change in Britain. Between 1962 and 1982 the average number of children per couple declined from 2.8 to 2.2, whilst over the same period Japanese life expectancy reached the highest in the world (by 1985 it was 80.2 for women and 74.5 for men). The arrival of labour saving devices in the home gave women with children at school much more free time with resulting increases in women returning to work and in female interest in matters such as social education. A series of Diet Acts demonstrating the changes in women's status were passed in the era of economic expansion such as the 1956 Prostitution Prevention Law, the 1965 Widowed Mother and Child Welfare Law, the 1968 Basic Consumer Protection Law, and the 1972 Working Women's Welfare Law. By

1984 national women's organisations had a total membership of 9 733 976 (about 23 per cent of the female electorate).

Greater affluence has reinforced Japanese interest and priority given to various forms of educational and cultural investment. by the 1980s the number of public and private libraries had reached 1642 whilst there were 676 museums. There were 11 096 full-time library staff and 8379 full-time museum staff. By Western standards Japanese interest in the monuments of the past during the 1960s and 1970s seemed casual. The age of economic expansion at any cost meant that industrial development always won out if historic buildings or a beautiful landscape got in the way. A city of stunning elegance like Kyoto continues to tear down its marvellous wooden domestic architecture to replace it with modern concrete and brick replacements. The new accommodation may be better to live in, but is much uglier. The Japanese keen eye for beauty does not extend to its new cityscape which, like so much Western architecture of the 1960s, 1970s and 1980s, is remarkable only for its ugliness. The major historic buildings are now somewhat safer under the Protection of Cultural Properties Law, but as yet the Japanese do not seem imbued with the West European determination to save the beautiful from the overwhelming power of economic development. The Ministry of Education, Science and Culture has an active policy of improving matters through such measures as 'providing maintenance and protection for important buildings, paintings, craft products and other works of cultural value; designating and preserving historic sites, places of scenic beauty and other sites of cultural importance; and encouraging the inheritance of traditional forms of drama and music, traditional craft skills, performing folk arts and so on' (Monbusho 1986 Report).

Such relative indifference to the environment during the 1950s, 1960s and 1970s demonstrated Japan's total commitment to economic growth, and ignored its pioneers in various fields of cultural development. After all, it was in the 1920s that Yanagi Sôetsu had created the folk art movement in Japan, and as early as 1931 the Japan Folk Art Association had resulted. Such pioneering in cultural matters has not always matched the Japanese commitment to economic growth.

In reviewing changes in Japan Professor Uesugi noted that, 'The role of the craftsman has been critical. Now young men and women are more interested in enjoying their leisure activities. Whilst it is necessary to avoid being a workaholic, Japanese industry will suffer some disadvantage as the country's skill base becomes weaker. However, Japan is looking to technological innovation to replace such lost skills. The differences between the qualified and unqualified are becoming wider. The number of craftsmen has declined as the young do not want to follow them. Japan is following Western Europe'. Reischauer confirmed (p.295) that, 'The Japanese have displayed since early times many of the characteristics that have contributed to their modern economic success. One was their tendency to work hard. Another was their drive for formal education. Others were the painstaking effort they displayed in their workmanship and their skill in mastering difficult technologies. Although they were introduced to agriculture and the casting of bronze and iron relatively late, they quickly caught up with the continental lands that had known agriculture for millennia and metalworking for centuries'. In the nineteenth century Europeans noted the high level of technical skill achieved by the Japanese in porcelain, metal-working, and woodblock printing. Much of Japanese economic success during the headlong expansion of the 1960s and 1970s was based on the work of skilled craftsmen in tiny firms. A city of industrial importance such as Osaka is composed of 48 000 factories, most of which are small. Zaibatsu giants of the interwar years such as Mitsui, Mitsubishi and Sumitomo (financial, commercial and industrial combines) may have been seen as malign symbols of Japanese imperialism, but their production was based on supplies from hundreds of small, independent workshops. This tradition continued after the Second World War and American efforts to put an end to zaibatsu.

The former skilled artisan who made possible such a small firm tradition now prefers to continue his education with hopes of university and the following white-collar job. Again, this is an international trend in the developed countries. Japan, as elsewhere, is aware of its danger and has attempted to modify its impact, such as by the introduction of colleges of technology in 1962. However, to the young the disadvantages of the small company as an employer are more obvious than the advantages. The tiny firm must use its manpower to its fullest extent as against the ability of the big company with many thousands of employees. As Professor Hiraki pointed out, 'Large and small companies are very different. In the latter you give less time to the company, but that is not possible in a small firm which must have your total commitment if it is to be competitive'. Despite Margaret Thatcher's attempts to encourage small businesses perhaps the future will inevitably be more like Britain than Japan with the large company replacing fully the multitude of small ones, if only because it can afford the technology which replaces no longer available skilled artisans.

In 1989 the government announced its intention that Japanese living standards should overtake those of the United States and West Germany. This ambition is far from outrageous in the light of Japanese economic success, but it does imply a formal switch from the national priorities of the 1960s and 1970s. As we have seen, since the 1950s Japan has spent most of its energy on economic growth at all costs. Probably the government commitment to improving the standard of living is a recognition that the voters have already made that choice. If such is the case this will have a further impact on the educational system. The quite ruthless use of education in the 1960s and 1970s as an adjunct of the economy will be modified. In Western Europe and North America it was discovered from the 1960s onwards that many citizens saw greater availability of education as part of their access to one of the good things in life. Education, like acquiring a car or longer holidays, was a consumer good. Of course, most will continue to see initial education as the means of getting a good job. This probably explains why Japanese attempts to establish new universities such as Tsukuba (1973), which were meant to create more flexibility in higher education and to innovate in structure and curriculum, have left unchallenged in Japan the paramount position of conservative institutions such as the Universities of Tokyo and Kyoto. Those who attend the latter know they will do well in the job market, and so entry to such places remains the fiercest in competition.

The traditions which Japan inherited from the centralised feudalism which was challenged only after 1868, such as strong central government, high regard for education, a good skills base, outstanding inter-personal relations, and national conformity, suited well the drive for economic great power status from 1955 onwards. The discipline and self-sacrifice was long established. A willingness to accept low wages, and the need to save for an insecure old age made available huge resources for industrial investment. The Japanese tolerated a meagre social welfare system, high environmental pollution, and inadequate physical infrastructure to aid economic growth. Now the Japanese citizen expects his and her reward as various anxious

Westerners declare the country economically number one. How will an education system so geared to the needs of the economy cope with an infinitely more complex society during the rest of the twentieth century? For education 1955 to 1980 were the easy years as the objectives were narrowly defined.

7 Conclusion: Education in the 1980s and Beyond

The American economic miracle was created out of the British Industrial Revolution. The British watched with admiration at what had been made out of their original innovation. In much the same fashion Japan has surprised and impressed the United States by building upon its borrowings, since 1945, mainly from America. Like others, Japan as a superpower in the economic league has constructed its achievement on the accumulated genius of the past. Alas, its period in the sun, as history ruthlessly teaches, will not last forever. Great powers come and go. Who will be next? China, perhaps? A politically united Europe seems more likely. Does it matter? As Japan and Europe become increasingly alike, a more rapid process than is acknowledged, probably not.

Will the economic superpower Japan continue with its present education system which served it well during the years of rapid, if at times painful, growth? As we have seen, the government still gives high priority to the economic role of education, but the 1980s have supported debates and discussions suggesting changing educational priorities. The third era of educational reform is under way. Whether it will be as ambitious as those after the 1872 Government Order of Education or of the 1947 Fundamental Law of Education remains to be seen.

Rapid economic growth, the impact of the developments in science and technology, resulting changes in society, and the impressive take-up of education in Japan have left problems such as excessive uniformity in the school curriculum and methods of teaching, severe competition for places at the most renown universities, and some indiscipline in the schools.

Increasing living standards have encouraged a demand for life-long learning. And many of the social changes encourage further learning as part of the solution and response to such changes, as Professor Uesugi stated in his important research on 'Living Conditions and the Education of Older People: A Study of Older People in Osaka-City' (1987), 'In a society with a rapidly aging population, the problem of the aged person is also the problem of us all. The problem of the aged is so critical that it ought to be considered seriously by all of us'.

147

Because of such changes the government established a National Council on Educational Reform in August 1984. It was given three years to carry out its work of a long-term plan of educational reform. On 5 September 1984 the Prime Minister asked for advice on, 'basic strategies for necessary reforms with regard to government policies and measures in various sectors so as to secure such education as will be compatible with the social changes and cultural developments of our country'.

In its 'First Report on Educational Reform' submitted to the Prime Minister on 26 June 1985 the Council identified eight principles for underpinning any reform. More emphasis should be placed on individuality, certain fundamental subjects must be emphasised, creativity must be encouraged, and also thinking ability and the power of expression, there must be greater choice, the educational environment must recognise its humanity, a life-long learning structure for education must be established, Japan must recognise that it is part of an international community, and students must be taught to cope with an age of information.

The Council decided that the major issues this list encouraged them to look at over the period of their review were: the requirements of an education system for the twenty-first century, the organisation of a life-long education system, a countering of the ill effects of too much emphasis on a person's educational background, higher education's enhancement and the individualisation of institutions of higher education, the enrichment and diversification of primary and secondary education, improvement in teacher quality, coping with internationalisation, dealing with the information age, and a review of educational administration and finance. The British tradition is one of reviewing separate sectors of education by committee such as the Robbins Report on Higher Education (1963) or the Russell Report on Adult Education (1973). It has often seemed that the British educational systems lacked a similar review of the whole service by an independent committee (as against such work carried out by the ministries or parliamentary committees). The Japanese, with an admirable logic, sought an overview of their educational system and a masterplan for the future.

To counter some immediate problems the Council proposed reforms on university entrance procedures, broadening and making more flexible university entrance qualifications, the introduction of six-year secondary schools and a credit-system based upper secondary school. In response the Cabinet set up a Ministerial Conference for the Implementation of Educational Reform, and a Head Office for the Implementation of Educational Reform based at the Ministry of Education, Science and Culture. The government intended to put into practice the Council's suggested reforms. In April 1986 the Council submitted its 'Second Report on Educational Reform'.

The most important of the National Council on Educational Reform's documents is the 'Fourth and Final Report on Educational Reform' dated 7 August 1987. It is an attractive document which has much to say about the Council's outlook: 'In its deliberations, the Council always aimed at ensuring free and unrestrained discussions, maintaining its independence and autonomy. It also always attempted to inform the public of the progress of its deliberations, so that the discussion might be open to the public. The Council has striven to make its discussions profound by listening to the views of all segments of the population, and thus aimed to involve all the people in efforts for educational reform'. The Council also had a sense of destiny: 'After a hundred years of 'catching-up' modernization since the Meiji era, we are at the threshold of a major transitional period in the history of civilization. We are going to move on to a new age of internationalization, of further spread of information media, and of greater maturity of society, which has never been experienced either by Japanese people or by any other peoples'.

The Council had aimed at a new perspective in Japanese education: 'The forthcoming age will call for a re-examination of human civilization and of the way of life of human beings, and will keenly require the further flowering of diverse cultures and the recovery of humanity. Education has a great mission and social responsibility in helping us meet these demands of the times. Being fully conscious of this mission, those who are concerned with educational reform must restore mutual trust among different parties in the education sector for the sake of the future of Japan, as well as for the sake of mankind tomorrow. They must thus create fresh vitality and creativity in the world of education'.

For those in other countries who unfairly saw the Japanese as 'economic animals' the Report firmly signalled changes in Japan's priorities, 'Japan has passed through the period of "catching-up" modernization which started at the beginning of the Meiji era. Now it is about to shift from the stage of growth to the stage of maturity as an advanced industrialized nation . . . As regards the life style of Japanese, the needs of the people have been diversified, individualized and heightened, in the context of the improved level of people's living, increased leisure time, better social security provisions, longer and better schooling of people and so on. The characteristics of 'affluence' in life demanded by Japanese people are going to change drastically as follows (1) from material affluence to mental affluence; (2) from quantitative affluence to qualitative affluence; (3) from emphasis on 'hardware' to emphasis on 'software'; and (4) from uniformity and homogeneity to more diversity and to the expansion of freedom of choice'. The list makes a dramatic contrast to education's priorities during the period of rapid economic growth in the 1960s.

The changes which Britain has experienced are now increasingly familiar to Japan. The Report makes mention of the impact of urbanisation with its loss of a sense of communal solidarity and diversification of values. The arrival of the nuclear family is part of the changes in the role of the home which have weakened traditional social norms. Notable during the period of economic growth has been the decline in the influence of the father. The new stresses have added to the burden of mental and physical ill health. The creation of a mass society has also introduced a mass culture which is often disappointing in quality.

The rapid development of science and technology demands actions to make sure it is in harmony with human beings. Fields such as life science and information science directly impinge on the quality of life. To be more creative in science and technology the Council considers it vital that there is greater exchange with the international community. The need for high talents suggests policies which will enrich higher education and promote basic research in the physical sciences, and also the humanities and social sciences. In this con- nection the Report warns, 'it is undeniable that modern rationalism, which provided an important impetus for the development of science and technology, has tended to neglect the importance of human sen- timents'. As Japan has absorbed both oriental and occidental cultures over many centuries it is important that it retains the strengths of both and encourages 'harmony between science and technology and human sentiments and sensitivity'. If the Japanese succeed in such a balance Britain and the West will have much to learn from them.

The Report gives much space to the increasing interdependence of the world. Japan, if it is to remain an advanced economy, 'cannot survive in isolation from the international community with regard to any aspect – natural resources, energy, industry, education, culture, and so on . . . Japan's efforts have so far been focused on importing

and transplanting science and technology from advanced industrialized countries in Europe and North America. It has not always
made adequate efforts with regard to the international exchange and
contribution in the fields of education, research, culture and sports'.

The Council proposes new perceptions and approaches to enable
Japan to produce a balance in international exchanges, and ensure
that it makes a proper international contribution. A greater number
of foreigners are to be encouraged to come to Japan and the Japanese
to go abroad more; 'the increased exchange of persons may cause
what is called "cultural frictions". Such frictions, however, should
be considered as normal phenomena in the international community.
Japanese people are urged to have a new and positive life style in
which they should convert these cultural frictions into forces for
internationalizing Japanese society. Through these endeavours, the
distinctive characteristics, as well as the universality, of Japanese
tradition and culture will be rediscovered and recognized anew,
and the Japanese culture will be able to contribute to the creation
of the peaceful and prosperous international community based on
co-existence and cooperation among diverse cultures and among
pluralistic systems'.

Turning to education itself the Report confirms that Japan's 'modern educational system has become a driving force for the social and
economic development of the nation, and greatly contributed to the
improvement of the people's living and culture'. But the present
system has a number of problems and severe limitations. Six major
areas of concern are listed:

(1) 'the principles such as the full development of personality,
respect for individuality, and freedom, which are emphasized in
the educational reform after the Second World War, have not
necessarily been fully established in Japan. There are many people
who are lacking in proper understanding of Japan's distinctive
tradition and culture and who have no adequate consciousness of
being a responsible member of a nation and a society. There has
grown a tendency that children's discipline and moral education
are neglected, and a proper balance between rights and responsibilities get lost'.

(2) 'The content and methods of teaching in schools tend to be
uniform, and many people too often insist on extremely formal
equality. There have been no sufficient efforts to identify and
develop the personality, abilities and aptitudes of individuals.

Excessive competition in entrance examination has led to too much emphasis in education on students' scores on standardized achievement tests, and on their factual knowledge. Much value has been placed on a good memory rather than on creativity, thinking ability or the power of expression. The phenomena of 'desolation' in education such as school bullying, children's rejection against attending school, and student violence in schools have begun to attract people's attention. The uniformity, rigidity and closedness of formal education have caused various ill effects'.

(3) 'Respective universities lack distinctive individuality with regard to their educational programmes. There are rather few outstanding educational or research accomplishments which have obtained international esteem. Scientific research in Japanese universities has so far very often tended to emphasize practical application of science to technology in particular. From a global perspective, Japanese universities have made little contribution to the development of pure science or basic research. Further, Japanese universities are in general closed, and they are too rigid and inflexible in carrying out their functions to respond adequately to social or international demands'.

(4) 'The social climate in which too much value is placed on the educational background of individuals has had adverse effects in the form of students' competition for better educational background with the aim of entering "prestigious" universities and famous industrial firms'.

(5) 'The uniform and rigid system of educational administration is hindering the activation of education to some extent. In addition, educational administration agencies are lacking in sufficiently flexible and positive attitudes to cope with new demands for a wide range of educational activities outside formal schooling'.

(6) 'After the Second World War, a climate of mistrust and confrontation was created in the education sector partly because some Teachers' unions unduly intervened in political struggles and in policies on school curriculum'.

Despite its successes the Report saw the education system as having lost the confidence of the public and failed to change with the times. It sought a full development of mind and body. The spirit of the 1947 Fundamental Law of Education needed to be more deeply rooted in Japanese soil. The Japanese should aim at self-determining spirits, public-minded characters, and those able to live competently in the world community. The National Council saw the move away from uniformity and the attendant emphasis on individuality as the most important educational principle. The Japanese priority of memorisation needed to be replaced by creativity, thinking ability and powers of expression. The Report reflects the sort of aims and objectives which made up the British educational system's values from the nineteenth century onwards.

Added to a model which emphasises liberal education is a recognition that any modern system has to be life-long. 'Thus we must ensure an overall reorganization of the structure of our educational system, with the shift to a life-long learning system as a core element'. Such life-long learning will need to make the Japanese less insular as the global village becomes the reality. With such changes of emphasis must come an upgrading of institutions and research. A long-term perspective regarding results must be taken. And in such developments as information literacy the benefits may be recognised, but also the disadvantages must be countered.

The First, Second, and Third Reports had made a number of concrete reform proposals. These included how firms recruit employees; the exchange of people between educational institutions, the community, and firms; the broadening of indicators of evaluation; reform of the vocational qualifications system; firms to end the practice of recruiting from only a small number of universities; more promotion from amongst the existing workforce; the influence of the home in education to be emphasised; more and better parent education; more counselling services; 'urban children should have an opportunity to live in rural areas, and rural children in urban areas'; Parent-Teacher Associations need revitalising; adults should have easier access to universities, upper secondary schools and other institutions; more flexible learning and entrance requirements; degrees by credit and community access to educational facilities and functions; 'community centres to conduct training and research for the promotion of industry in the community'.

> Voluntary learning activities contribute to making people's lives fulfilling and worthwhile . . . Therefore, the following measures should be taken: the development of a network for learning information; development of appropriate structure for the presentation of relevant information and for counselling services; the provision of government assistance to non-governmental programmes in education, sports and culture; the cultivation of a sense of

community through learning activities; the expansion of opportunities for participation in social services, in the form of voluntary activities, by offering training programmes; the recruitment of an adequate number of leaders for the education of adults and out-of-school youths, and the improvement of the quality of these leaders; and the utilization of new media in non-formal education programmes.

Vocational training centres should be set up and off-the-job programmes for employees encouraged; sports should be promoted with a national Consultative Committee for the Promotion of Sports; communities should become 'life-long learning towns', initially with national and local government selecting certain municipalities; facilities must be improved for life-long education; universities should be permitted to develop distinctive structures in research and education; credit accumulation systems to be encouraged; a drastic reform of graduate schools to be pursued; post-graduate provision to be strengthened in staff, facilities and equipment.

The Council proposed replacing the Joint First-Stage University Entrance Examination by a Common Test to be used voluntarily by universities; educational guidance at secondary schools should be improved; a major review of research structures to be implemented and more post-doctoral felowships provided; international exchanges to be developed; wider recruitment of teachers should include foreign nationals; university teachers to be evaluated and the possibility of limited terms of office explored; universities to be more deeply involved in educational provision for their communities through public lectures, extension programmes, more working adults as students, making available their facilities, and the dissemination of information; in elementary schools 'stress should be placed on enabling children to master the basic skills of reading, writing and arithmetic and to develop good social attitudes and aesthetic sensibilities'; textbooks should be reviewed to promote diverse approaches to teaching; an in-service training programme for new teachers should be established, such teachers to have a first year of training after their appointment; throughout their careers teachers should undertake regular in-service training; very large schools should be eliminated and the maximum class size reduced; the appointment of relatively young teachers to administrative positions to be encouraged, and principals should have their duration of service lengthened to maintain a school's vitality and discipline; schools should eliminate corporal punishment; the government should prepare a paper on the internationalisation of education; the attendance of a Japanese student in a foreign secondary school should be seen as the equivalent of attendance at a Japanese school; schools with foreign students and/or Japanese students returning from abroad should have a specialist teacher to counsel them and their parents; more foreign students should be accepted in Japanese universities and the system modified to accommodate them; foreign languages, and notably English, should be encouraged; pre- and in-service training of Japanese language teachers needs to be revised; to aid information dissemination high-quality software should be developed for education; 'The University of the Air . . . is of a great significance from the point of view of developing higher education utilizing information media'; open data bases should be created; more importance for private schools with distinctive aims or principles; more power of decision given to local government; a review of many areas of private education encouraged (for example, the desirability of juku or crammers).

The role of the private education industries in life-long education needs to be explored; high value industries which are knowledge intensive should be promoted; greater rationality in educational finance sought, with ways of relieving excessive family expenditure on education to be explored; the Ministry to recruit more experts and strengthen its research function; the 'authoritative posture' of some of the Ministry's officials needs to go; with regard to local boards of education' . . . the Council proposed in its second report, the following measures need to be taken: selection and in-service training of board members; introduction of a definite term of office for the superintendent of education and the making of the municipal superintendent of education a full-time post; establishment of a mechanism for sharing responsibilities for dealing with grievances; dealing with teachers not suited to the teaching profession; improvement of the efficiency of business management of education boards in smaller municipalities through cooperation with neighbouring municipalities; and cooperation with prefectural governor's offices'; the school year should begin in the autumn, not April.

The concluding three and a half pages of the Fourth and Final Report are devoted to stressing the importance of the implementation of educational reform ('The destiny of Japan in the twenty-first century will be greatly affected by whether this educational reform will be successfully brought about or not'). In January 1989 the

Ministry of Education, Science and Culture reported to the forty-first Session of the International Conference on Education on 'Development of Education 1986–1988'. This permitted the government to say what progress had been made in meeting the calls for educational reform.

One of the most notable changes in a Japan preparing for the last decade of the twentieth century and the first of the twenty-first century is the Ministry's loss of complacency. For an institution famed previously for its conservatism it is remarkable that its review holds such statements as, 'We should constantly strive to reform the educational system, envisaging what our society should be in the coming years'. The Ministry's summary of the four Reports of the National Council on Educational Reform states, 'the most fundamental ideas for the current educational reform are, firstly, to carry out actively the transition to a life-long learning system, secondly, to develop educational programs in which emphasis will be placed on individuality, and, thirdly, to make our education system cope with such changes of the times as internationalization and computerization'.

The Council's recommendations have inspired considerable governmental response. In September 1987 a University Council was established to advise the Minister on higher education matters. During February and March 1988 the Ministry submitted six bills on educational reform to the National Diet. So far three have been through parliament, resulting in the creation of a multi-disciplinary graduate school, changes in the National Centre for University Entrance Examination, a new system of induction training for beginning teachers, the diversification and greater flexibility of upper secondary education, and the switching of some authority from the Minister of Education to the prefectural boards of education. The following session of the Diet is to deal with a review of 'the existing categories and standards of teacher certificates and to enable people working in other sectors to be employed as teachers'; 'To make municipal superintendency of education a full-time position. To introduce a specific term of office for the superintendent of education'; and 'To set up an Ad Hoc Commission for the Implementation of Educational Reform as an advisory body to the Prime Minister, with a view to helping promote relevant government measures to be taken to meet the recommendations of the National Council on Educational Reform'.

Other proposals of the Council required amendments of Cabinet Orders or Ministry of Education, Science and Culture regulations.

So far changes here in June 1988 saw the abolition of the Ministry's Social Education Bureau and the creation of a Life-long Learning Bureau, the Division of the Sports Department into a Sports-for-All Division and an Athletic Sports Division, and the combining of the School Lunch Division and the School Health Division into a School Health Education Division. In February 1987 amendments were aimed at improving the training of social education officers. This was followed in May 1987 by new rules permitting chairs and research units to be donated to national universities. A system of credits for upper secondary schools was agreed at the same time as recognition of credit equivalence for secondary school study abroad. As early as September 1985 an amendment saw the award of university entrance qualification to graduates from upper secondary school courses of special training schools, and in July 1986 to those who had completed a regular course at a seaman's school. In January 1987 work was begun on introducing a national system for the training of physical education leaders in communities. In June 1988 amendments aimed at a national system for the training of sports programmers were agreed.

The government agreed extra funding for change; 'In the Ministry's budgets for the fiscal year 1988, a total sum of approximately 767 billion yen was allocated to various activities related to educational reform. This amount represented a 7.2 per cent increase over the previous year'. The Ministry strove to develop an infrastructure for life-long learning at prefecture and municipality level. More money was allocated to open up institutions of higher education and upper secondary schools. Improvements in the school curriculum were financed, and experimental induction training programmes for new teachers. A maximum class size of 40 in primary and lower secondary schools was agreed. In the private sector Ministry money has been directed at aiding 'unique and highly demanded educational and research projects'. Extra financial assistance has been given to foreign scholarships. Computers and other information equipment has been made available to schools. Training programmes for teachers in the field of information processing have been established. Learning resource information systems have ben developed by the Ministry. The prefectures have received a number of guidance circulars from the Ministry on subjects within the Council's recommendations, such as how to deal with bullying and how to promote sports activities. The bureaucratic hand of the Ministry has been less obvious in the running of state universities (for example, over the appointment of university teachers). There has been better public information on educational decision-making. In January 1988 the Ministry published 'The Implementation of Educational Reform – The Current Situation and Future Issues'. In June 1988 this was followed by 'The Development of International Understanding and Cooperation – Through Various Activities in Education, Science, Culture and Sports'. In December 1988 came a White Paper entitled 'Government Policies in Education, Science and Culture in Japan'. In April 1988 the magazine *Newsletter of the University Council* was launched.

The proposals of the National Council often demanded the development of greater detail through advisory committees. In December 1987 the Curriculum Council reported to the Minister of Education on national standards for the curriculum of kindergartens, primary schools, lower secondary schools and upper secondary schools. This resulted in the Ministry issuing revised courses of study for kindergartens, elementary schools and lower secondary schools in late 1988, and for upper secondary schools in 1989. The Educational Personnel Training Council gave its views on teacher training in December 1987. Other Councils have dealt with everything from the promotion of life-long learning to the construction of more intelligent buildings for educational and cultural institutions. In July 1988 the Ministry began a large-scale reorganisation of its structure to enhance its efficiency in promoting educational changes. It also began exploring the changes needed to enable the school year to begin in the autumn.

Many of the changes listed above to a European or North American look like further evidence of Japan catching up. The desire for smaller class sizes or better in-service training for teachers has been on the British educational agenda for many years. The clear emphasis given to a system based on life-long education is a stage further on than some European countries like the United Kingdom. Whilst Plato talked of the need for life-long education in *The Republic*, British governments fear that a formal recognition that we are in the age of having to see education as being needed from birth to death may imply spending more money. Other West European states have acknowledged this reality for several years, and spent extra money on it.

Because of its insularity it was inevitable that Japan would have to make internationalisation a key issue in educational reform. As the world finds technological developments bringing people ever closer the Japanese aloofness looks ever more costly. But whatever the reasons for placing internationalisation near the top of the education agenda this does make a contrast to our own Little Englander system.

As in other areas of life, the Japanese are throwing themselves into educational reform with energy and official commitment. After economic success based on a closely allied and rather unattractive educational service, they now aspire to a more broadly-based system which gives the highest priority to creativity and innovation. They are aware that such educational sophistication will be needed to move on to the next stage of economic development as places like South Korea and Taiwan displace them in manufacturing cars and electrical goods. In the meantime the British system is gearing up to produce the style of conforming citizen who served Japan so well in the 1960s.

I have a delight in walking around Kyoto. After visiting a temple in late April 1989 I was on the elegant shopping street of Shijo Dori when a small, badly shaven and somewhat untidily dressed man joined me. In impeccable English he began our conversation by telling me his age which was 76. Without asking, he had assumed I was British. I responded by saying how beautifully he spoke my language. He then explained that before the Second World War he had been taught by a lady from London: 'She was the best teacher I ever had, very strict and correct'. As we strolled, before he left me at a bus stop, he explained that he had been conscripted into the Imperial Navy during the war and had seen service in China and Southeast Asia. At the bus stop he said, 'Good-bye, old boy' and slapped me on the chest.

Besides enjoying yet another unexpected and entertaining meeting with a local I was left wondering if the Japanese are yet ready to see their 'very strict and correct' educational system modified. Nobody likes change, although people of ambition have to pretend to. Would the Japanese cling to an institution which had helped them achieve the sort of growth unparalleled in other economies? Would they risk their children's future to a new, unknown educational system? Creativity, innovation, internationalisation are meaningless words compared to the promise of a guaranteed good job if you conform and perform well in the existing system.

Whilst not all citizens are demanding change, the government has used some signs of popular discontent to promote at least a major modification of the education service. They know that the next model of economic success will be built on the foundation of a workforce which is highly educated and creative. Since 1868 central government has largely determined what happens in Japan, despite Japan's present system of parliamentary demoocracy. Educational changes will be put into effect because the government has decided that they must be. A mature manufacturing economy has continuously to keep at least one step ahead of the next industrialising country.

Index

161